Perfect Daughters

Perfect Daughters

Revised Edition

**Adult
Daughters
of
Alcoholics**

Robert J.
Ackerman, Ph.D.

Health Communications, Inc.
Deerfield Beach, Florida

www.bcibooks.com

Letters in chapter 1 reprinted with permission from the authors.

After a While. Reprinted by permission of Veronica A. Shoffstall. ©1971 Veronica A. Shoffstall.

Excerpt from *All I Really Need to Know I Learned in Kindergarten* by Robert L. Fulghum, copyright ©1986, 1988 by Robert L. Fulghum. Used by permission of Villard Books, a division of Random House, Inc.

Excerpt from *I Am an Adult Child of an Alcoholic* by Thomas W. Perrin. Used by permission of the author.

Keeper Hole by Alison Snow Jones. Reprinted by permission of the author.

Library of Congress Cataloging-in-Publication Data

Ackerman, Robert J.
    Perfect daughters : adult daughters of alcoholics / Robert J. Ackerman.—Rev. ed.
      p. cm.
    Includes bibliographical references and index.
    ISBN-13: 978-1-55874-952-8 (tp)
    ISBN-10: 1-55874-952-7 (tp)
    1. Adult children of alcoholics—United States. 2. Daughters—United States.
    3. Codependency. 4. Adjustment (Psychology) I. Title.

HV5132 .A265 2002
362.29'23—dc21

2002024342

Publisher: Health Communications, Inc.
        3201 S.W. 15th Street
        Deerfield Beach, FL 33442-8190

R-04-07

Book Cover Design by Andrea Perrine Brower
Book Inside Design by Dawn Von Strolley Grove

To Lydia and her daughters
Kimberly, Mary and Debbie

Other Books by Robert J. Ackerman, Ph.D.

Children of Alcoholics
Same House, Different Homes
Let Go and Grow
Too Old to Cry
Before It's Too Late
Silent Sons
A Husband's Little Black Book
A Wife's Little Red Book
Growing in the Shadow

 Author's Note

The cases and experiences shared throughout this book are real. The names and identities have been changed to ensure confidentiality.

 Contents

PART TWO
Collecting Emotional Baggage

PART THREE
Codependently Yours

PART FOUR
Concerns of the Day

PART FIVE
Discovery and Recovery

Acknowledgments

Many people contributed to the writing of both editions of *Perfect Daughters*. I am grateful to all of them. For the first edition, I would like to thank (again) Judith A. Michaels, Edward Gondolf and Charles Bertness for their support and research skills in the development of the adult daughter questionnaire and data analysis. Linda Sanford and Diane Glynn were encouraging and supportive and gave me the push to start the book. Thank you to Marie Stilkind for her editorial assistance.

For the revised edition of this book, I would like to thank Christine Belleris, Susan Tobias and Lisa Drucker for their editorial help. I want to thank my graduate assistant, Jacquelyn B. Griffin, and Crystal Deemer for her administrative support.

For both editions of this book, I wish to thank Peter Vegso of Health Communications for undertaking this project and for the many successes that we have had together. To the person who has listened many times to the thoughts and concepts on these pages, Kimberly Roth Ackerman, thank you for all the seasons.

Finally, I wish to thank all of the adult daughters who have contributed to this book and to the lives of so many others. I admire your willingness to share parts of your lives in order to help other women with parts of theirs. Thank you.

 Preface

Since I wrote the first edition of *Perfect Daughters*, some things have changed; some things have not. Several things, fortunately, have changed for the better. Foremost is that more help is available today for children of all ages who grew up with one or two alcoholic parents. Educators, counselors, therapists, youth mental-health workers, clergy, legislators and many others are now more aware of the many issues facing children of alcoholics. Also, many excellent programs have emerged to help. These programs now exist at the national, state and local levels.

Another change is that getting help for being a child of an alcoholic, or an adult child, is more acceptable. Clinicians are better trained to help with the issues of alcoholism and the family. I believe, too, that the approach to helping has changed for the better. We are more likely to use a strength model to help, to recognize adult children as survivors, and to build on the resiliency skills that many people developed as young children. No longer are we treating children of alcoholics as victims.

Especially relevant to this book are the many changes that

women have made for themselves and for others. Although not all the changes that need to be made for women have occurred, as social changes have been made, women are in better positions today not only to seek and receive help, but also to help other women. This change has greatly increased the likelihood that more adult daughters of alcoholics will find needed help and support.

What has not changed is that we continue to produce parents who develop alcoholism and that children grow up in addicted and other types of dysfunctional families. Additionally, we still have more untreated alcoholics than recovering ones, which means that most children of alcoholics will still grow up in a family with an alcoholic parent who continues to drink. Thus we still need to provide help for children of alcoholics, regardless of whether or not the alcoholic parent finds help.

Another situation that has not changed according to my perception is that adult daughters of alcoholics still continue to lead the way for helping not only children of alcoholics, but also adult children. I still hear and see more adult daughters than adult sons who are willing to share their stories, insights, fears and strengths in order to recover and improve the quality of their lives.

Finally, one thing that definitely has not changed is my own passion and desire to help other children of alcoholics. My soul still shouts "Yes!" when I know that somehow I have been fortunate to help someone, and I can see in their eyes that their self-doubts are being replaced by positive self-esteem. Since my first book, *Children of Alcoholics: A Guidebook for Educators, Therapists and Parents*, back in 1978, I have been blessed to be part of a growing movement to build a community of people who want to improve the quality of their lives. The journey has been magnificent, and I am not finished yet.

This new edition of *Perfect Daughters* contains updated information. I have added new sections on resiliency in childhood and adulthood, a new section on high-risk relationships, "Afterthoughts" at the end of each chapter, and two new chapters. The Afterthoughts are quotes from famous women that I hope will leave you thinking about yourself.

The first new chapter contains letters from perfect daughters that I have received since the first edition of the book. Some of the women who wrote the letters asked questions; some shared their stories of successes; others shared their pain; some wanted to say "thank you"; and some just wanted to connect and say "hello." As you will see, their letters introduce us not only to other perfect daughters and their issues, but also to all the topics covered in the book. I've placed these letters first.

The second new chapter, "Secrets and More Secrets," addresses some of the most common issues for many adult daughters, which unfortunately occurred in their own homes in addition to the alcoholism. Parental divorce, abusive behaviors and eating disorders are covered in this chapter. These issues, which have things in common with each other as well as with parental alcoholism, all contribute another aspect to an already difficult life for many adult daughters.

I hope that this book and the many insights shared by adult daughters will help you. You deserve it.

 Introduction

Since the mid-1970s, I have had the privilege of participating in one of the most rewarding, emotional and unique experiences that I could imagine: involvement with children of alcoholics of all ages and with the children of alcoholics movement in our country. I have traveled all over this country lecturing, speaking, sharing and listening to and about children of alcoholics. This is truly a grassroots movement in all respects, about children of all ages who experienced pain in childhood, but want love, joy, health and beauty in their lives. The movement is about recovery.

As I have observed and participated in this coming together of millions of previously silent voices, I have observed two things. One is that the children of alcoholics movement has been swept off its feet by generations of adults who were raised in alcoholic families, "adult children," who are now leading the way for the generations after them. Two, the overwhelming majority of these adult children who are willing to lead and to share parts of their lives in order to help others have been women. Most children's issues have benefited as a direct result of the women's movement in this country, and the children of alcoholics movement is no exception.

During my travels I have had the opportunity to listen to many women who were willing to share their stories; these stories started my interest in adult daughters of alcoholics. Their willingness to express feelings, ideas, pain, insights and recovery has opened the door for many women and men who have lived in the isolation and silence of alcoholic families. I am indebted to all of the adult daughters who helped me understand them better and thus convey to others what I have learned. If you are an adult daughter of an alcoholic, this book is directed at you, for you and about you.

This book is based on research and interviews with women from alcoholic and nonalcoholic families throughout the United States in hopes that it will provide insight and understanding, not only for "adult daughters of alcoholics" themselves, but also for those who love them, live with them, work with them and support them.

More importantly, this book is about recovery. Not all adult daughters are affected in the same ways, nor do all have the same issues. All of the daughters in this study, though, shared the desire to better understand themselves, their behaviors today and ways they can improve their lives. The issues they shared ranged from understanding their personality characteristics and behaviors as adults, relationship and intimacy problems, relating to their parents, their own parenting skills, working through childhood feelings, their addictions, sexuality and a desire for recovery. Perhaps some of these concerns are yours.

This book is divided into five parts. Part One includes a new collection of letters received over the years from adult daughters of alcoholics. The first part of the book also explores childhood by revisiting many concerns about how an alcoholic parent raised you.

Part Two considers the different relationship dynamics and effects that occur when the daughter is living with an alcoholic mother as opposed to an alcoholic father. Part Two also includes a new chapter that addresses abuse, eating disorders and divorce as they relate to the life of an adult daughter.

Part Three is about understanding yourself and many of your behaviors. Additionally, we examine the source of many of your behaviors and how many adult daughters have adapted specific behavior patterns in their lives, both positively and negatively.

Learning to accept your past, your present behaviors and most importantly yourself is the focus of Part Four. Topics in this section include adult daughters' opinions on relationships, parenting, issues with their own parents and working through their own addictions, if any.

Part Five addresses discovery and recovery for adult daughters. As you read this book, and hopefully develop a better understanding of yourself, you will be discovering yourself. Am I saying that you do not know who you are? No, but I am asking, how well do you know yourself? Do you know all of the parts of you, your behaviors, and why you think and act the way you do? In discovering who you are, have you reached a decision on the parts of you that you would like to keep, those you would like to discard forever and those you would like to change? Have you discovered your fears, doubts or perceived limitations? Have you also discovered your strengths, talents, capabilities and abilities to improve the quality of your life?

As you read this book, you will see the words of many women and the many common themes expressed. However, please keep in mind this underlying theme about all adult children: All of us are survivors. I am tired of listening to and reading books and articles about adult children of alcoholics as if we were the most incredibly dysfunctional adults ever created. I don't know about you, but I have never met an adult child who does not consider herself or himself to be a survivor. Yes, the lives of children of alcoholics include much pain. If you look closely, though, you will see that you have many skills and much potential. I am writing about the survival, hope, capabilities and strengths that I have witnessed and heard from adult survivors. I am not writing about the despair and hopelessness of victims. The many women in this book overwhelmingly echoed that they are survivors.

The study that this book is based upon drew on a national sample of 1,209 women in the United States. Of these, 624 were raised in alcoholic families, and 585 were raised in non-alcoholic families. In order not to interrupt your reading or your thoughts, all statistics and tables are in the Appendix. In addition to the study, 200 women who were raised in alcoholic families agreed to interviews. Their insights, comments and personal stories provide the emotional reality about the lives of adult daughters that research data alone could never convey.

In writing this book, I have faced a great challenge in that I am not "authoring" this book, but rather I am facilitating the words that have been shared. I have called upon my skills as a researcher, writer, counselor, adult child and—most importantly—listener to convey to you what I have heard. I hope that I have listened well and that the two goals of this book—a better understanding of adult daughters and providing choices for recovery—will be met. I also hope that my goals as a writer facilitate your goals as an adult daughter.

Part One

Childhood Revisited

Chapter 1

Am I the Only One Who Feels This Way? Letters from Perfect Daughters

We're all in this together—by ourselves.

Lily Tomlin

Most people like letters. A good letter lets you know that someone was thinking about you and took the time to say hello. Since writing the first edition of *Perfect Daughters*, I have received many letters from adult daughters of alcoholics. The content of their correspondence has included sharing their life experiences, asking questions about themselves, wondering if being raised in an alcoholic family affected them, concerns about their relationships, wanting to know how to let go of the past, offering hope for other adult daughters and, finally, just saying "thank you."

Most importantly, however, these letters are from women who are no longer in denial about their lives, who are taking charge of their recovery and realizing that they are not alone. Experiencing pain and trauma can also lead to becoming inner-connected with others. Some of the letters that I have received make up this first chapter. Although each letter came from a different source, they obviously all share common themes. I share these letters with you here in hopes that you, too, can feel connected. I thank my correspondents for writing these letters and for letting you know that you are no longer alone.

Dear Dr. Ackerman,

I wanted to write you after reading *Perfect Daughters*. It was the first book I read on children of alcoholics in its entirety, as I find most self-help books not very helpful at all. . . . I especially liked that the book didn't fall into the all-too-common trap of making any and every behavior out to be codependent.

In reading *Perfect Daughters*, I realized I have made a lot of progress. I also realized I have a long way to go, as I am still in a lot of pain. Mostly I feel stuck in that I've been in therapy—have learned a lot about myself and why I act in certain ways—and yet I don't know where to go from here. It's as though I've realized intellectually how screwy my upbringing was, but I haven't worked through it emotionally. I still have a great deal of anger. I still have a lot of fear in relationships. It is hard for me to feel truly close to people (men and women). When I get scared or vulnerable, I tend to cut people off. I have close friendships, but it's hard for me to feel like they are really close. At times I become afraid, and then I tend to isolate myself because it feels safer that way. Sometimes I find it is easier to be alone, but then I get confused because I am naturally introverted and reserved—so I don't know how much of my being alone is just my personality and how much is related to my upbringing. And I constantly question if I am "normal."

I think accepting myself is a large part of recovery, but as you pointed out in your book, it is not enough for me to *know* this. I have to *feel* it. How does one do this? I'm still not clear on that. You also advise to learn about "letting go." Can you tell me how you do this? Do you just tell yourself, "Let go," or what exactly does an individual need to do to let go? I have yet to come across any material that explains the "how to" of letting go. Also, my situation is different from the other daughters in your book. Not only did I have an alcoholic father, I had a chronically mentally ill mother who was extremely emotionally abusive. Are there any books about growing up in this type of household? I think it might be similar to having two alcoholic parents, but I'm not sure. If you have any information that would be useful, I would greatly appreciate it. I have tried a number of ACOA meetings, and generally I do not like Twelve-Step programs. Are there other alternatives to the Twelve Steps that would provide support in a group setting? Again, any information you could provide would be appreciated. I am glad I came across your book. I'm sure it has helped many adult daughters. Thank you so much for your time in reading my e-mail.

Sincerely,
Elizabeth

Hello Dr. Ackerman,

I am twenty-five years old with a father who's been in recovery for eighteen years. Until I read *Perfect Daughters*, I did not realize I was still trapped in codependent hell. I've always referred to myself with a smile on my face as "Daddy's little girl." The fact of the matter is, my father is and will always be an alcoholic. Today, I can say with my head held high (I'll work on the guilt), I am no longer his codependent.

I found your book by accident . . . just by coincidence (God's way of staying anonymous—that'll be the only cliché, I promise). . . . My father at fifty-three is going in for triple-bypass surgery tomorrow. This is the first "normal crisis" for my family, and what a bunch of wackos we are! For the first time in my life, I can see us through the eyes of a semi-healthy person, not just an adult daughter. I've cried this week, and it felt great.

I am coming to terms with the fact that I cannot fix anyone else. My mom, dad and brother are on their own. I care about ME.

That's a little background. I am e-mailing you first to say, "Thanks!"

Second—just to mention that although parents get sober, not everyone else in the family goes into recovery at the same time. My father has been sober since I was seven. Like I said, I am now twenty-five. Don't get me wrong; I know that because of his sobriety and MY and my husband's skills, we are able to maintain a healthy marriage. My best friend has an active alcoholic father and she cannot. (Don't worry, I sent her your book.) I now have the marriage my parents never did. Thank God!

So anyway, I am strong. I am learning to stand on my own two feet. I can't believe the one relationship in my life that I thought was the best is actually the worst.

Thanks again—you are a very special man!

Jen

Dr. Ackerman,

Thanks so much for asking me to relate some of my ACOA experiences. I agree reading about others' experiences helps us. I know that it gave me a lot of hope when I read about other women whose experiences were even worse than mine and how they eventually learned to manage their lives without allowing the behavior of the alcoholic or chemical-dependent in their lives to drive them crazy.

I am thirty-seven years old and became a widow at the age of twenty-three. I have been in my current relationship for fourteen years now. I am the oldest of four siblings and the only daughter. At nineteen I married my high-school sweetheart, James, who also came from an alcoholic family. We were living overseas while he served in the military, and he was killed in an auto accident. Our marriage was on the verge of breaking up at the time of his death because he continually cheated on me.

I met Brian just a few short months after that. He showered me with attention that I so desperately needed at that time in my life. A part of me was sad that my husband had died, but another part felt such relief now that he could not hurt me anymore. I think I'll always feel a little guilty for feeling that way, but it truly is how I felt.

Brian was a bit of a partier when we met, but we were young and single and had no children, so it didn't seem like a problem. For years after we first met we would get together with friends and drink socially without any adverse effects. We were just young and having a good time. The problems began about seven years down the road when we decided to start our family. It was a no-brainer to me that you just buckle down and grow up when you make this decision. It was not that simple for Brian. I did not realize that substances were a real addiction for him. It became worse when he started experimenting with crack cocaine. He would use and stay gone all night long. This was going on during the time I was pregnant with our daughter. I can remember being eight to nine months pregnant and driving around town in the wee hours of the night on countless occasions looking for him, when I should have been home asleep because I had a job to go to the next day.

I would stay awake crying all night long. It was a miserable time in my life. I would call his mother in the middle of the night and complain to her, which she did not especially appreciate. Once I was so fed up, I gathered up all of his belongings and made them into a huge pile and plopped them in the middle of the living room floor with the intention of making him move out as soon as he came back!

Since the birth of our daughter, the incidents are fewer and farther between, but he still relapses. I think it's been a long time since he's used crack, but I know he still occasionally smokes pot, and he will use alcohol to excess. It still upsets me when he uses, but I finally did realize and have accepted that it is always just a matter of time before another incident. I used to think that someday he would grow up and outgrow all this irresponsible behavior. Now I understand that he probably won't. Alcoholism and chemical dependency are not problems that you simply "outgrow." However, I still find it very frustrating when he comes home after one of his nights of partying and tells me how angry he is with himself and how *this time* is different, and that he really is going to change and never do it again. You can imagine how many times I have heard him say those words.

In the beginning, I would believe him, and things would be okay for a while and then, of course, it would happen again. Then more promises, only to be shattered. I no longer have it in me to believe them anymore. I'd really be crazy if I did. It just hurts too much to allow myself to believe it, and to brag to my friends and family about how *this time* he really means it, that *this time* is different. They would always look at me, and I knew what they were thinking: "How gullible she is." I'm tired of feeling like a fool, and it just hurts too much to have all that hope shattered over and over and over again. So now I just accept that this is the way he is.

I suppose I consider myself grateful because things could be worse, much worse. He could be a mean, raging, violent alcoholic who drinks every single day and makes the lives of everyone in the house a living hell. That's the way my father was. So, no, I suppose this doesn't seem so bad. Brian can go months, even a year or more, between relapses. It creates the illusion that maybe he finally did succeed this time. Until just this week, it had been more than a year and a half since his last relapse.

He left the house to take my brother home, who by the way is an alcoholic as well, and did not come home for about four hours. It was a twenty-minute drive. He called several times that evening to feed me excuses about why he wasn't home yet. I knew all along that he was up to no good. The incident before that, a year and a half ago, he had also been with my brother, and to make a long story short ended up in jail that night. He called me to come and bail him out. I told him no way; that there was absolutely no way I was going to drag our children out of bed in the middle of the night to bail him out of jail. I pointed out that he had gotten himself into the mess and he could deal with it. Why should I suffer for it? He sat there all night long. It was one of the best decisions I ever made. Brian even admitted that himself. It gave him a lot of time to think about his life and what might happen if he didn't get his act together. So, yes, I know I am doing much better than I was a few years back. I know I have what it takes to take care of me now.

My biggest worry now concerns our children, especially my daughter. We have two children together, a daughter who is seven and a son who is four. I know that as our daughter gets older she will begin to sense the tension in her parents' relationship. Eventually Brian will pull one of his stunts and she will find out about it. I am not going to lie to her about it. I won't do that. She'd see right through it anyway. Children can tell when you don't really mean what you say, or when you're sugar-coating something. I know I always could. I don't ever want to send her such confusing messages. As a matter of fact I feel that Brian should have to explain that to her. But then, and this is my biggest fear, I know she will eventually come to me and ask me why, when he lies to me and behaves the way he does, do I stay with him? That's a tough question. It's even tough for me to answer, even to myself. Of course I love him, and he is a wonderful father. He's a good person in so many ways. Our daughter just loves him. Our son is a bit more withdrawn from him. He has never really been comfortable around men in general. I worry about how she will react when she finds out her daddy is not perfect, and I worry that she is going to get the message that it is okay to stay in a relationship with someone who lies to you and treats you in a way less than what you deserve. After all, that does appear to be what Mommy is doing.

I want so badly for the chain of codependent women to stop here with me, and for her to be as emotionally healthy as possible, and my son, too, for that matter. It is more difficult for me to imagine how this is all going to affect him at this point. I obviously can relate best to my daughter. I do remember reading that boys do often draw on how their fathers treated their mothers when they begin to learn how to relate to the women they have relationships with.

So I continue to work on my recovery. I have to because I know that I fit the mold of the "adult daughter." I used to have a bad habit of trying to fix the rest of my family, too—my three younger brothers who are all chemically dependent or alcoholic, and my mother, who of course was very codependent to my father. My parents finally did divorce once all of us were grown, and my father died only a few years later alone in his apartment from diseases caused by his many years of alcohol abuse and smoking.

I believe my mother feels disappointment at some of the lessons I have learned so well from my recovery journey. It upsets her when I say that I hope my brothers eventually get their lives together, because I do not consider it my responsibility to take care of them when she is no longer around to do it for them. I will not be a caretaker to them and make it easier for them to continue drinking and using. She, of course, does not see it that way. She feels I'm being too hard on them, and how could I treat my own family that way? They have to learn at some point in their lives how to take care of themselves. It's not my job to do it for them. It reminds me of one of the ACOA slogans: "Didn't Cause it, can't Cure it, can't Control it." I live by those words now. It was such a struggle in the beginning trying to accept that, and to learn to let go and stop trying to control everything and everyone. At the time, I just could not imagine how that could work. I was certain that all that control was the only thing keeping my life, and the lives of everyone around me, together and sane. But it finally sunk in that if I just let go, and started taking care of me, that everything and everyone else would, one way or the other, take care of itself, and that that was okay. Things did not always work out the way they would have if I had taken control, but what a relief it was when I was finally able to distinguish between my life and my responsibilities and those of everyone else. I truly could not tell the difference before. If you had a problem, it was mine to fix. Simple as that. Patty to the rescue! Not anymore. I still struggle with what life dishes out, but I know I'm a lot better at dealing with it than I was ten years ago, and I'll continue to grow in my recovery and be better yet ten years from now.

Thanks for all of your wonderful books. They truly have made a difference in my life, and I appreciate the opportunity to share some of my experiences with you and with others who are on this recovery journey. Thanks.

Patty

Dear Robert,

I grew up in a family with two alcoholic parents. I never learned to trust my own perceptions, my feelings, the truth or myself. My father would come home from work and bring up a beer from the basement refrigerator even before he greeted us. My mom wouldn't start drinking until we were in bed. The liquor was kept out of sight in the bottom of their bedroom closet. It's still there today.

I remember the fights in the middle of the night. As the youngest of three children, I was the only one who would get up, intervene and try to fix it. I must have been five or six the first time I begged my father not to kill himself.

This particular time, I remember lying in bed and hearing the murmur of their voices ebb and flow over Johnny Carson's. I agonized over when to get up. If I got up too soon, they would deny they were fighting and the interruption would just prolong their drinking. If I timed it right, I could persuade them to go to bed.

This night I knew I'd waited too long when the fight moved into their bedroom. My dad threatening to leave, drawers slamming, jamming his feet into his shoes, getting the car keys, calling my mother names I'd never heard before. The blaming, the cursing. I tried to block my six-foot, three-inch father from leaving the bedroom. With no more thought than swatting at a gnat, he moved me aside. Then he started spewing his self-hatred: "You'd be better off if I was dead. I'm going to kill myself. I'm no good. No one loves me."

And me begging, "I love you, Daddy. Don't. Please don't. Come back. Don't go." And my mother, as always in denial, saying, "He doesn't mean it. He won't do it."

And he went halfway downstairs. And just before he would have left our sight, he stopped. And for the first time, I saw my father cry. His sobs echoed through the foyer. And he sat on the steps with his head in his hands. It was over. Until next time.

In the morning, my father ate his two eggs with me at the breakfast table in our usual tense silence. We pretended nothing happened. To this day, we've never talked about it. As a twenty-something newspaper reporter, I interviewed two women addiction counselors. They described the various roles in an alcoholic family and how alcohol abuse hurts everyone. I saw my family and myself. It took more research, more years and other counseling before I went into counseling to understand and accept myself as an ACOA.

I'm nearly finished with *Perfect Daughters*—again it's reassuring to see how far I've come. Yet, I know I have far to go. At least I am ready and willing to work on areas of my marital relationship that are unhealthy. I'm no longer in denial about this. It won't be easy, but he's trying. I'm not sure if we're with the right counselor, but he won't see anyone else and this counselor is also seeing my children. So he knows the whole picture.

I am still recovering. (Does it ever end?) I no longer live in denial. I'm not perfect, I make mistakes and the world doesn't end. I'm okay. I survive. I now follow my inner voice—not perfectly, but I'm listening. I still use work and busyness to avoid conflict in my relationship with my husband. But I detect when I'm doing it, try to find out why and speak up.

I worry about passing along the alcohol legacy to my children, but not as much as before. I seek help when I need it and experience less shame. I'm still learning about healthy boundaries.

Today, I am able to tell my eighty-year-old father I love him—and I mean it. I say it without strings and expectations. It is my gift to him—and to myself. It hurts that he doesn't say it back. I don't know why·he can't tell me, "I love you," but I realize that is his problem. He has loved me the best that he can. I am grateful he tells my children, especially my son, "I love you." I will never know why he won't say it to me. And that's okay. I no longer need his approval for my survival. I'm okay without it. I am learning to love and respect myself.

I am worthy of being loved and I deserve to be respected. Robert, it wasn't until hearing your talks that I realized why I still tell my dad I love him. I don't excuse him from what he's done, but I've forgiven and released the anger. His silence won't hurt as much anymore. His inability to tell me he loves me has more to do with him than with me. I still feel sad, but I'm moving beyond it.

Thanks again for the wonderful insights your work has provided me. I'm going to read *Before It's Too Late* soon.

Respectfully,
Patt

Dear Dr. Ackerman,

I know it's ridiculous, but I am so intimidated just writing this letter. I am an aspiring writer myself, but my experience as an adult child from an alcoholic family precludes everything else. I am ignoring my inner critic to send this letter off to you.

Your graciousness in asking me if I would consider submitting something for your revised edition of *Perfect Daughters* set off all those voices that continue to be a part of whom I have been in this life. I have learned, however, to listen to them . . . thank them for their participation . . . and then ask them to please sit down! Only after I go through this little ritual of mine can I find the courage to move forward.

Putting your address in my computer was the first step. That one took two weeks. The next step was this: sitting down and just going to it. It has taken me five more days to get to this. I am rejoicing at this moment in time. My recovery has brought me to this. I didn't even do college till I was thirty.

I am forty-three years old this year and in some ways I feel as if I'm just starting out: that sense of freedom a teenager has when they first leave home for school or that heart-pounding adrenaline that comes with taking a healthy risk with a good support system behind you. I was not born into a healthy support system, but I have learned enough over my years in recovery to have been strong enough to create my own—and it is the best. My staunchest supporter is myself. I have a relationship with a God that has a place inside me. I have learned to distinguish between the old self-destructive voices and the self-preserving one. Your work was a major stepping-stone for me. I thank all those women who went before me. I do regular speaking engagements and talk about the miracle of discovery as a result of the miracle of recovery.

My family was a regular at the well of trauma, and our most repeated lesson was that of "Don't trust that anything in life is good for very long or without a high price to pay." It has been a long road and I'm not dead yet, so I still have much to learn. Since they tell me the best is yet to be I have decided to stick around and test that theory. My life is wonderful these days with all the opportunity I see in front of me. I am trying on my wings; they have barely been used. I do hope you will consider writing back to me if you can find the time. Just writing this letter to you has been one of the highlights of my life so far.

Thank you for this line of communication with someone I so deeply respect. I will write to you again if it is not an imposition. Please let me know.

With sincere respect,
Maggi

Dear Dr. Ackerman,

My dad was an active alcoholic. My family talked quietly about my dad's drinking, but only my mom would speak to him about it. That speaking was usually silent smoldering until the volcano erupted. I remember being a very young child, four or five. The kitchen table was yellow—I spent a lot of time there, fiddling with my food. My mom would prepare the evening meal and it would be on the table every evening at the same time. My mother and I would sit and wait for my dad—who stopped at the tavern each night on his way home from work. We would wait. Supper got cold.

We would wait. When my dad finally came home, he would come to the table. The stony silence made eating the cold food impossible. So, I would spill my milk. Looking back, it must have been just to break the incredible tension. My dad would leave his meal uneaten and my mom would yell at me while cleaning up the spilled milk. I've spent much of my life spilling the milk in tense situations. I married a man, not alcoholic, but just like my dad. He is a runner—in many senses of the word. We were together for over twenty years and raised six children. I continue to be drawn to quiet, contained, distant men. I continue to see the possibility and think that I can live with the possibility in my own head. I continue to this day to struggle to stay in the reality that I see, rather than the possibility that I believe could happen. I'm better at seeing the flags sooner and sooner, and I'm getting better at listening to the wisdom I have gained, If it looks like a duck, and quacks like a duck, and walks like a duck—chances are *real* good that it's a duck.

I hope this will be helpful for other women. It is helpful for me to see it in print.

Nancy

Hi Dr. Ackerman,

I just finished reading *Perfect Daughters,* and I wanted to say "hello." After a lifetime of silence, I feel like I want to talk. I feel excited. Finally, someone understands my life. Now, if I can only understand it!

I am the oldest daughter of two alcoholic parents. I have three sisters and two brothers. As a child I always knew something wasn't right, and that something seemed to center around the beer bottle that was always there. I didn't like what it did to my father; I didn't like how it made my mother react to it, but most of all, I didn't like how it made me feel— mostly angry and confused.

I was fifteen years old when the first major crisis caused by alcoholism hit our family. The crisis was the first one that I remember that had a major impact on me. My mother's alcoholism and depression reached a point where she was hospitalized in a state mental institution for three months. However, at that time I didn't know those words. All I knew was my mother was gone, and my job was to handle the family responsibilities. My father never learned to deal with responsibilities or how to deal with crisis situations.

While my mother was gone, my father depended on me a lot and I was there. I helped keep the family together. The first week my mom was gone, different relatives had taken us all in. I heard talk of foster homes, so I contacted my dad and said he'd better get us home quick! I told some well-meaning relatives where to go in the process. I could now take the anger I felt for the bottle out on these people. Boy, did it feel good! I became known as the young lady with a chip on her shoulder.

Even as tough as I was, that period was a difficult time for me. School had always been my oasis and I had good grades, but during this time my grades plummeted. I went to a Catholic high school, and the nun guidance counselor called me in to lecture me about my grades. I happened to be in a very vulnerable state at that time, so I told her what was going on in my life. She said, "Oh, I didn't know." That was all; I was sent back to class. She gave me no comfort, no hugs, no reassuring words. I was crushed, humiliated and embarrassed. I had opened myself up for the first time in my life and was made to feel that what was happening in my life was unimportant. That experience helped to confirm my already growing feeling that I could only depend on myself to handle painful situations in my life. My dad was too weak to deal with them, my mom wasn't there, and my teachers just didn't care.

I didn't talk about my family's alcoholism again until seventeen years later—when I walked through the doors of Al-Anon's Adult Children of Alcoholics group. There I learned that all those times I felt something was wrong with me, there was. I was affected by alcoholism also. It was a disease, a family disease. I threw myself into this program, reading everything I could lay my hands on to understand alcoholism. I remember reading a book by Claudia Black that talked about "Don't talk, don't trust and don't feel." She said that families with alcoholism had these rules; in fact, they are more than rules, they are laws. As I read those words, I remembered my experience at school when I was fifteen. They are indeed powerful laws, but I was determined to change my way of life. Entering that ACOA group was the beginning of an amazing journey. I am eternally grateful to all of those who had the courage to take those first steps in helping us to learn how to break the silence.

You helped me, and I just want to let you know that.

Thank you,
Barb

Dr. Ackerman,

I attended one of your sessions on "Perfect Daughters" a couple of weeks ago at the recommendation of Beverly, my therapist. She suggested that I write you this letter.

I thoroughly enjoyed your session, and you might as well have been speaking directly to me. I have only been in therapy for a few months, so all of this is relatively new to me but so fascinating and right on the mark. I purchased your book and immediately read it. There, too, you were talking directly to me. In addition, I saw many traits in myself as the ACOA that I didn't even realize had any connection.

My father was an alcoholic, and my mother was very ill from the time I was born until she died when I was sixteen. Naturally, after that, my father's alcoholism escalated until he gave up drinking when he remarried (at which time I had been married for six months). Beverly has helped me to realize that I was neglected as a child due to his alcoholism and my mother's illness. Therefore, I turned to food as my constant companion and comfort and have become a compulsive overeater. I never knew why I was obsessed with food and could not relate my eating habits with any mood, etc. Now I understand. In addition, in reading your book I have discovered that I am codependent and display all of the character traits you mention for the daughter of an alcoholic father, as well as some of the alcoholic mother. As Beverly helped me to understand, even though only my dad drank, both parents were like alcoholics because my mother couldn't take care of herself—much less me!

Dr. Ackerman, thank you for taking an interest in this subject, writing books and speaking on this issue. You have opened my eyes to the "whys" I am like I am and you have given me a better understanding of who I am and where I came from, as well as where I want to go! I have lots of work to do on "me" but I am learning to love myself, and with God's help and information such as you have given, I will emerge a mentally and physically healthy individual.

Grace Ann

Dear Dr. Ackerman,

I just wanted to let you know that I only have a few pages of your book left, and it has helped me sort out so many feelings. I know I still have a long road ahead of me, but I also know that the worst is definitely behind me. Many of the things you pointed out, I already realized but just didn't know how they fit together with where I've been, where I'm at and where I'm heading.

I know that you have to be extremely busy, but I do have one question. (Okay, maybe two.) If you do not respond, I will totally understand, but I just have to ask. Through reading your book, I realized that I am among other things fighting for control in a somewhat controlling relationship that is currently unhealthy (actually it was always unhealthy; I'm hopeful that it can eventually become healthy) with a high-risk male. Is it probable that the relationship can be salvaged, especially since I realize I still have a lot of recovery ahead of me? Is it probable that I will be able to fully recover and become the person I want to be and know I can be in the above-mentioned relationship?

I hope that I will be able to have you sign my copy of *Perfect Daughters* someday.

Thank you once again for your time and for all the invaluable information in your book that has helped me learn about myself in the past, present and future forms.

Sincerely,
Autumn

Dr. Ackerman:

I've been listening to your taped lecture on "Perfect Daughters" this week just to try to get back in touch with the reality of my issues and why the issues exist. I fit so well into the descriptions you give for the daughter of an alcoholic father. When I first read *Perfect Daughters*, long before going into recovery, I knew that you had met me through your interviews with women around the country. That's when the connection began for me, even though I had never met you. You were telling the world about me in your book and suddenly I didn't feel quite so alone because the secrets were out for the public.

A part of me wanted to lend the book to my mom, but she was not open to the idea that my personal problems had anything to do with her. I had to hide my pain from her, and the only way I could do that was to use drugs and alcohol. Mental-health therapists were available only to the insane in my small town. Besides, if word went out to the community that I wasn't functioning appropriately, my mother would abuse me even more. I had no one to talk to about who I was, so I lived inside of myself and created an internal world that kept me from leaking my pain.

Being in recovery has been confusing to me. If I trust my

internal world and keep to myself, I eventually end up on the psychiatric unit. But when I expose my thoughts and feelings, I feel so frightened. I'm vulnerable. I wonder who is going to hurt me. Nearly every woman in my life becomes my insensitive/ codependent mother; almost every man becomes my father figure.

I've been walking around this last week in a fog so thick that I only trust the path I've had to take in the woods of my internal world. In there, I run from the hostile *Wizard of Oz* trees. I rest next to the body of a hibernating bear. I shiver in the cold rain and I walk barefooted on the muddy trail. And I think of how wonderful it would be to relive the childhood that I want today. I want to be the daughter of parents who love me unconditionally because they choose to. I hope I can get better.

Sincerely,
Lois

Dear Dr. Ackerman,

Growing up with an abusive, alcoholic father left me very needy and vulnerable. I guess it was obvious all along. I was just never able to recognize or admit it.

When I was young, less than about ten years old, I think that I probably wanted my father's approval and love. After about age ten or eleven, though, I began to realize how awful my father was. I realized that he drank too much; my friends began to notice and make comments. I was humiliated, embarrassed and ashamed. I also realized that all of the fights my parents had were his fault. I didn't want to have anything to do with him or my sick family. I'd leave the house and pre-tend they weren't my family, but actually they controlled my life.

Looking back, I realized how much time and energy I devoted to daydreaming and imagining that I would be res-cued, accepted and loved. I didn't want approval (I was very competent with lots of achievements) as much as I wanted to be loved and to believe that I could be loved. I wanted a loving family, and I wanted to believe that I could be loved by a man as a daughter. I wanted a father so much that it consumed me. I yearned for that love and sense of security and protection.

I eventually became very tired—tired of life, tired of the pressure and stress of having to be perfect and taking care of everyone else. I was tired of having to rescue my mother and brothers and sister from being abused. I wanted to be taken care of, and I wanted to be rescued. I wanted someone to show me that they cared about me. Everything was so confused.

All through my college years, this yearning for the love of a father never went away, and it was all confused with my other needy thoughts about being rescued. All of these feelings and thoughts were in me. My neediness made me vulnerable and blind.

Then a guy came along who claimed to be able to fill these needs. I became a child, as if part of me was reliving that childhood pain and fear and sought to be rescued from it. I felt like he was rescuing me and I wanted to believe it. I let my childhood fantasies of having a loving father control my adult life. I saw myself as helpless. He convinced me that I was helpless and that I needed him, which wasn't hard for him to do. Something in me became a child—needy, unable to make my own decisions, afraid and wanting to be rescued.

I let myself be controlled by him because of the emptiness and hurt that I wanted to go away. I wish I had known that by being controlled by someone else, I became less and not more. My hurt and loneliness became bigger. I actually knew how to take care of myself and make decisions, but I was tired. Before I knew it, I was in a terrible situation that I couldn't get out of for a long time. It was a nightmare.

I know that some people can be trustworthy, but I also know that some people look for others to hurt and use. Their reasons for acting this way aren't my problem or concern, but taking care of myself is.

I guess I would want to warn other women not to make the same mistake by letting their needs and vulnerability control their decisions. Unfortunately, I wasn't aware that this was happening until it was too late. I wish I would have known that this could really happen to *me*. Some close friends who had known what was going on in my life would have helped, too. They would have seen things more clearly and would have been able to warn me, but I didn't know how to have good, trusting friendships. The isolation I was in helped this person to be able to use and abuse me and keep me under his control.

I wish I knew then what I know now. I do know, however, that your book has helped me tremendously. Thanks for writing it and for reading my letter.

Fondly,
Joann

Dear Dr. Ackerman,

I'm not sure why I am writing to you. I don't want any answers. I guess I just wanted to write to someone who understands me. I hope you don't mind. I never realized that my alcoholic father controlled me. I thought I was the "chosen one" in the family to have escaped his angry ways. No one could penetrate the bond that I had with my father. I was confused and weary at times when I would witness him beating my mother, but I knew not to cross his path and by doing so I was shown the love he could not show towards my mother.

My childhood had many chaotic moments. I watched my mother lie knocked out cold on the kitchen floor from a punch by my father. My father never hit me, but soon it was my turn to feel the brunt of the beatings from my mother and two older brothers. Even though I was a child at the time, I had the sense to protect myself from them by befriending my alcoholic father. He cared for me when they could not show their love for me. The father-daughter relationship I had with him was very special, and I found solace in learning from the simplicity of its genuine love.

My father and I enjoyed the sport of alpine skiing together for years. We raced father-and-daughter events all over the state and won and collected ribbons and medals. What made skiing so fun for me was to have my father ski with me as a partner, watching me as I improved my skills and teaching me new ones. If I fell on a racecourse, he was there to pick me up and brush the snow off me, always telling me not to give up. He was so supportive of me. Today, it is hard to believe that he was probably a full-blown alcoholic at the time and unable to relate to the adults in his life. I know I am defensive today when I talk about my father, but he was the only person in my family who really knew me and loved me.

My first drink was with my dad at the age of five or six, sipping beer from his bottles that I would get for him from the refrigerator every night. That was part of the routine, beer and crackers for my drunken dad before supper. The more serious drinking I did began when I was a teenager because I could not handle the stress of seeing my alcoholic father's health deteriorate. I watched him turn into a street person, a man with no purpose but to consume alcohol and roam around town in tattered clothing. When he finally died I was seventeen. At that point in my life I couldn't handle my grief either, so my answer was to drink more alcohol. I never intended for it to become a "problem," but it did.

I am consistently questioning who I am, wondering if I'm okay, and always attempting to accept my strengths and weaknesses. I find myself seeking approval from the men in my life more than I do the women. I have a valley of lows and a mountain of highs. Medication helps, but not to the extent of allowing me full freedom to be the person I want to be. I can't be the gorgeous model or the money-making executive. I'm the recovering alcoholic living vicariously through the eyes of a "wannabe."

Life is interesting with a dual diagnosis of "alcoholic" with "bipolar illness." I fought being labeled for a long time, partly because I did not want to believe I was either. But a day came along when I relapsed after being six years sober and I felt the insanity of both illnesses. My madness grew into rage towards God. No recovery tool I felt comfortable using that afternoon could curb my irrational thoughts. Plain and simple, I hated my life. I feel fortunate to have not died that day, knowing what I know today as a recovering adult daughter of an alcoholic.

My life as a daughter of an alcoholic was one huge secret. What happened in my home on a regular basis, utter chaos, was never revealed to friends or teachers. I lived two lives. At home, I was a soldier in a war. In school, I was a mischievous little girl buying time in a safer haven where no one asked me what was going on at home. But as the wars continued, I began to want my teachers to care a little bit more. Though my grades were good, my classroom behaviors were uncontrollable. I spent many afternoons sitting in jacket closets or out in hallways alone, wondering what would happen that night between my parents. Would Dad come home drunk again? Would my mother harass him and cause a fight? Whose side would I take? Life was so complicated. I didn't understand it for a moment. I seemed to only get along with my dad. Why didn't I feel safe with my mother? I felt hated by my mother and two brothers. So Dad and I chiseled out a childhood for me that consisted of skiing, playing softball, hiking, going to the beach, basketball camp, taking long drives in the convertible, watching plays and eating out. All the destruction from the domestic wars was put aside once we stepped out of the house together. My mother raged with jealousy as she watched us leave every day; she never received any positive attention from my father. No hugging or kissing, no tenderness or love. Just broken promises and physical pain.

My brothers felt that their father abandoned them; I was not a popular sibling with them. When I was not with my father or at school, I was a target of bitterness and anger. My mother saw the bruises and the scratches on my body, but she seemed to think I deserved them. When my brother broke my hand during a ritual beating, she yelled at me and delayed taking me to the hospital for hours.

I learned to become a tough little tomboy by age seven or so in order to protect myself. I also had an imaginary family in my mind that I kept to myself for years. This family encouraged me to sing songs from the musical *Annie* (I had bright red hair) out in my front yard in hopes to be "discovered" and be in movies. I also wanted to go to the Olympics as an alpine skier, and my imaginary family members cheered for me through every downhill race I entered, win or lose. Such a world of make-believe helped me to isolate and survive by keeping the secret.

My parents finally divorced. I was nine, and with no explanation other than "he didn't want you," I lived with my mother and brothers. The wars continued, but my dad wasn't there to protect me anymore. My behaviors at school worsened and my teachers finally began to investigate the homestead. What they found was nothing more than the normal sadness of divorce; they empathized with my mother. I wanted so badly to tell them the truth about my family, but I maintained my loyalty as I had been taught to do. Eventually, my childhood ran away from me.

When you grow up in an abusive home, you have no sense of safety. I used to climb up this enormous tree in the front yard just to get away from everyone when an argument or fight broke out. Usually I wouldn't be followed, so I had the privacy to cry if I needed to. I stayed wedged up amongst the limbs of the tree for a few hours counting the cars going by, singing songs to myself, whittling a branch with my pen knife until my mother would come out and yell for me to "come down this minute." Sometimes I did, sometimes I didn't. The tone of her voice usually made that decision for me.

Despite the family problems and the poor attitudes I

brought along to school, the amount of resiliency that I portrayed each day was remarkable. My grades were good. Each season I prospered at playing a sport, and I belonged to extracurricular clubs. I spent weekends and summers with friends who were goal-oriented. Sure we experimented with drugs and alcohol but we were fortunate not to have landed in any trouble over the years that we did those things. I vented but without telling the family secrets, so my friends had no idea that my dad was a chronic alcoholic.

They also did not know about the conflicts I encountered with my codependent mother. My friends liked my mother because she appeared "cool." Obviously, my mom put on a good act in front of them. We both kept our secret. So to look at my life from the perspective of a teacher or a coach, I would see Shelley's life as a rather stable one. In actuality, I felt as though I was struggling to keep my head above water. I worked hard at these tasks to seek attention from my parents; everything I achieved was done for them. It didn't take long for me to lose control once I went off to college to be on my own.

I graduated from high school without an acceptance into a college for the following semester. Why? I hadn't applied to colleges. No money was ever put aside for my future. Besides, I barely got through my senior year. I didn't know how to grieve the recent deaths of my father and older brother. I hid my pain and was "strong for my mother." That was the rule in our household. I look back at that year, and I feel so much anger towards my family and teachers for not taking better care of me. Why didn't they realize that I was playing a part in a horror movie directed by God and my mother? I was seriously depressed and no one really appeared concerned. All eyes were turned on my mother and how she was dealing with the loss of her son. I appreciated that. My parents had divorced years before my father's death so she was not so sad about his dying. My main concern turned toward my mother because I didn't trust she could take care of herself. I didn't want to lose her as well. I sacrificed a noticeable part of my young life that year taking care of my mother and not myself. I needed to read *Perfect Daughters* back in that year of 1981.

Thank you for writing it.

Sincerely,
Shelley

Hello,

I was at one of your workshops a couple of weeks ago. Your work always makes me very emotional. I spend days processing.

I am an adult daughter of an alcoholic father. I am also an incest survivor, a recovering alcoholic, codependent, drug addict, sex addict and workaholic. I have recovered from anorexia and compulsive spending. I have been married three times and had two more long-term relationships with men, all of them unhealthy. I am thirty-seven, the mother of two, a case manager for people with disabilities.

Having said all of that, what makes me saddest about me is the guilt I still feel taking any time for myself and the almost compulsive way that I constantly feel I must work on me. God, do I need a rest!

If you want, I am happy to correspond. I have always enjoyed and hated your work. Please take that in the way it was written, with humor.

Sincerely,
Kelly

Dear Dr. Ackerman,

My name is Christina. I am a reader of your book, *Perfect Daughters*. Doing something like this is rare for me, but I had to write you and thank you for writing that book. I will keep and read this book more than once to keep up on recovery. I am twenty-four years old and single. My father and mother were both alcoholics. My dad divorced my mother when I was three years old. He went sober up until a year ago. My mom was not a part of my life, and she died when I was sixteen. Up until I started seeing a counselor about six months ago, I had no idea what was wrong with me. I felt lost, lonely, tired of trying so hard in relationships and wondering why I still felt so empty.

My dad was my savior. He never talked about his alcoholism, I heard about it. My mom was always to blame. Now, at fifty-eight years old, sober twenty years, he's at it again. I thought my world was going to end. I never remembered him being drunk, only my mother. I've come to find out in my healing that I don't have the father-daughter relationship I thought I had with him. I am looking at it realistically now, not how I did as a child. I've changed my outlook anyway. Three or four years ago I found myself angry with my father, and I'd ask myself, *Why?* Alcohol was not found in our house from when I was four years old up until I moved out at nineteen. You know, it's terrible—my dad stopped drinking for nine weeks after his last downfall. He's back again and hasn't worked for four days. (He has his own business.) But his girlfriend called and told me. I said, "What do you want me to do about it? I can't save him or watch over him. I love him, he's my father, but I'm going to take care of Christina now, something I haven't done the whole twenty-four years I've been around." Your book has inspired me. It's scary, sad and a relief. I'm not in denial, though—you can't be if you want to truly change. I've never had a serious boyfriend. I've always wanted a healthy, meaningful relationship with a man and wondered why I didn't have one. I take on men unavailable in some way, shape or form and push away the guys who are ready to get to know the real me. Before that can happen I lose interest, and that's something else I want to change.

I know I can do this. I'm still young, single, attractive, no kids, and I'm ready to take on the world. I feel so good now that I know why I felt so out there and lost for so long. Now, I know why. Once I can change, I can't wait. I want to go back to school eventually. I'd love to counsel children or be a speaker, anything of that nature. I'd love to counsel kids before these terrible patterns became habit—prevent the habits before they became ACOA.

Again, thank you, thank you and thank you!

Sincerely,
Christina

AFTERTHOUGHTS

*If there's a book you really want to read, but it hasn't been
written yet, then you must write it.*

TONI MORRISON

I hang my laundry on the line when I write.

JONI MITCHELL

Life resembles a novel more often than novels resemble life.

GEORGE SAND

*Better to write for yourself and have no public,
than to write for the public and have no self.*

CYRIL CONNOLLY

*I write for myself and strangers.
The strangers, dear Readers, are an afterthought.*

GERTRUDE STEIN

Chapter 2

Home Groan:
Daughters in
Alcoholic Families

Once upon a time, a little girl lived in the kingdom of child-hood. She was known as the "princess." Her kingdom was the same as all other kingdoms, she was told, and she wanted to believe it. However, she often found it difficult to understand the royal messages, which didn't always make sense to her. Could something be wrong with her? Maybe she wasn't like other girls. Why couldn't she understand what she saw and heard? She wanted to believe that she and her kingdom were perfect. After all, she was the princess.

I know, she thought, *I will make it all right and perfect for everyone and then nothing could possibly be wrong.* So the princess spent her childhood making all the things in the king-dom that were wrong appear to be right.

This task was not easy for her, but she never complained. Besides, whom could she tell? She was a princess and a pro-tector of the kingdom. When she did ask questions of mem-bers of the royal family, she was told, "What are you talking about?" or "Don't worry about those things. Little girls are supposed to be happy." Well, if that was what little girls were supposed to do, then she would do it. She would show everyone that she could do it better than anyone else could and be the best little princess ever.

No matter how hard she tried, the royal messages were still unclear and they did not stop coming, especially the ones that she received from her parents, the king and the queen. You see, the king and the queen did not get along very well. Outside of the castle and in the presence of their royal sub-jects, the king and queen pretended that they were the best royal couple in the kingdom.

The king, however, was not always so perfect. In fact, much of his behavior confounded the princess because he was a confusing king. Some days everyone in the kingdom loved him, and some days, especially when he drank wine, everyone hid from him. He even treated the princess differently sometimes. Some days he told her he loved her, and on other days he frightened her.

Oh, well, she thought, *I guess that is what kings do.* Besides no one said anything bad about the king. He was more like an emperor, and no one wanted to tell him about his new clothes.

I know, thought the little girl, *I will tell the queen about the king. Surely she will understand and help me.* But, alas, the queen could not see things clearly either. She had learned to pretend, too. After all, she was once a princess herself. The only things that she told the princess were, "Life in the kingdom is hard. Don't say anything to the king or his subjects about drinking wine, and besides, some day you will find a prince who will take you away from all of this."

Now more confused than ever, the princess had another idea to help her understand her childhood kingdom. She decided that the real reason those things appeared different, but really weren't, was because she lived in a *magic* kingdom.

That's it, she thought. *This is an illusion. This isn't really happening, and if it isn't really happening, it will go away. What will go away? You know, the things that aren't really here.*

Soon the princess began to feel better because she began to think like everyone else in the kingdom. Now she got along better, even with the queen. She learned the magical game and became part of the inner codependent kingdom.

The princess was smarter than other people in the kingdom, however, but she couldn't allow others to know what she knew. She became very good at the magic games and kept her feelings buried in a secret place. The hiding place was so good and so secret that soon even the princess forgot where it was and what was in there.

The years in the kingdom passed, and the girl became an expert in her royal role of "perfect princess." Mixed royal decrees were still everywhere, but she kept them in her heart, always wondering what they really meant and who she really was.

What happened to the little girl in the kingdom? She grew up and became a woman.

I wasn't allowed to cry when I was a little girl. That was noise my dad didn't want to hear. He'd tell you to swallow it or he'd give you something to cry about. Well, I feared him so I would fight back the tears. I wouldn't allow myself to be afraid as a child and would turn it into something else. I would go to my room and make believe, pretending that I was a princess living in a castle and everything was okay. Now, when I look back on what my childhood was like, I feel the fears, I feel sadness, I feel hurt and I feel anger.

Growing up in a dysfunctional family where both of my parents were alcoholics, the screaming, yelling, fighting and arguing seemed to me to be normal. That's what normal was to me. It was easy to deny any problems because I lived in a fantasy illusion that this happened in everybody's house. That way I could survive it.

You know, I'd go to a girlfriend's house and I'd see differences from the way things were in my house. I'd leave and say, "Oh, things are the same way at my house. They just don't do that when people are around."

My mother used to drink. I'd come home from school and she'd be passed out. To me, she was napping, and that's how I denied that my mother was an alcoholic. Or if I came in and she was drinking and I had brought a friend home, we'd make a joke about it. I'd say it's cocktail hour and it's okay. It took years to accept the fact that my mother was an alcoholic.

I never knew how much it had affected my own life or even if it had affected my life. When my mother told us that her drinking didn't bother anyone, I believed that. Not until a few months ago—when I couldn't explain the depressions that I'd been going through for the past six years, or when I couldn't make my therapy sessions because I just didn't have the will to go—did I know that something was deeply wrong with me. When I couldn't be consistent in my work and with the things that I wanted to do with my children, I knew I had a problem. And when I woke up one morning and I just wanted to die inside, and death was easier than the pain, then I went for help.

Donna

Does Donna's story or the story of the princess and her kingdom remind you of yourself or your childhood? If so, you might be one of millions of women who were raised in an alcoholic or other type of dysfunctional family. Although you may feel unique or isolated about your childhood experiences, you are not alone. In fact, more than 22 million adults in our country were raised by one or two alcoholic parents.

For those of you who are aware of the children of alcoholics movement in the United States, you know that children of alcoholics who are now adults are referred to as "adult children of alcoholics," or "adult children" for short. Women who were raised in alcoholic families are referred to as "adult daughters" and are the focus of this book. If you are unfamiliar with the names or the movement but have lived the experience of having an alcoholic parent, welcome.

The adult children's movement is concerned with two processes: growth and recovery. Growth is dependent upon understanding, accepting and working through the experiences of your childhood. Recovery allows you to go beyond your childhood experiences and become the type of adult woman you would like to be. Although you may have had a negative childhood, you can recover and have a healthy, positive adulthood.

Can you identify with the many adult children who have become part of this movement? For example:

- While you were growing up, did you secretly feel that you were different from the other girls? Do you still feel different today as a woman?
- Are you the type of adult daughter who has many unresolved issues from your childhood?
- Do you feel that something is missing in your life, but you don't know what it is?
- Are you incredibly competent in some areas of your life, but you feel vulnerable in other areas?
- Do you have relationship problems and are always attracted to the wrong people?
- Do you secretly try to hide your low self-esteem?

Your answers depend upon your childhood, how significantly you were affected, how you cope today as a woman, and how well you understand yourself and your desire for recovery.

All of these questions and answers can sound overwhelming, particularly if you believe that your childhood is over and therefore no longer affects you. But do you have problems today, yet you're not sure of the source? Are you really different from other women or other adult daughters?

Family: Your Museum of Memories

In my childhood I was not allowed to express anger. I was only allowed to express happiness and joy. That was acceptable. Anger, sadness and frustration were not acceptable. The only way that I could be accepted by my parents was to be perfect, to look perfect, to act perfect, to be happy and to be the model child.

Jill

Some adults can't remember much about their childhoods. However, for some the problem is they can't forget it. Many adult daughters have very vivid memories of growing up. They can remember past events as if they happened today. Others say that they cannot remember much and have blocked out many childhood memories. Still others begin to remember the episodes and emotions of their childhoods as they begin to talk about them more.

Many adult daughters who say they do not remember much are concerned that their lack of memory means something is wrong with them. Many people block out unpleasant memories in their lives. If you do not remember all of your childhood or cannot recall everything, don't worry. After all, you don't have to have a perfect memory, too!

As you recall your alcoholic family, I am sure that you will experience mixed feelings, which is appropriate since most alcoholic families frequently send mixed messages to their children, such as, "I love you, go away," "Nothing's wrong, but don't tell anyone," or the unspoken message, "Please emotionally deny what you physically see and how you live."

Many of your mixed feelings and perceptions are based on your observations that your alcoholic family was not totally one way or the other. No dysfunctional family is totally negative or without some good times. On the other hand, even healthy families have some dysfunctional behaviors or stressful times—except, of course, if the Cleaver, Anderson, Nelson, Brady or Huxtable family raised you and you visited your cousins, the Waltons, on weekends. Maybe you remember as a child comparing your family to TV families and wishing your family could be like them. Surprise: Many children who were raised in "normal" families made the same comparisons.

We were and are a "looking good" family and giving up that fantasy has probably been the most painful part of my recovery, but it's also where I've experienced the most growth and freedom.

Mary

In your alcoholic family, you were probably exposed to both negative and positive behaviors from other family members. Unfortunately in alcoholic families, as in other dysfunctional families, the negative experiences usually outweigh the positive ones. Thus your mixed feelings occur when you remember both the good and the bad. You might remember how your father behaved when drinking or how he could be verbally abusive. Yet, this same man might have told you how beautiful you were and called you his special daughter. You may feel contempt for the alcoholism, but love the person. You might have trouble admitting that your mom was alcoholic because, after all, this is *your* mother that you are talking about and saying negative things about her isn't easy.

Although I know my mom had a drinking problem and it most likely played a large role in her death, I still cannot admit verbally that my mother was an alcoholic. I don't want and didn't want my mom to be an alcoholic. My mom was too special to be an alcoholic. I don't think I will ever be able to admit this fact.

Candice

Obviously what affects you negatively today about your childhood are the negative experiences. Ellen Morehouse, cofounder of the National Association for Children of Alcoholics, tells us that—regardless of the type of alcoholic who lived in your family—most young children of alcoholics experience fears and concerns in at least seven areas in their lives while growing up a child of an alcoholic (1982). These fears and concerns include:

1. Worrying about the health of the alcoholic parent
2. Being upset and angry at the unpredictable and inconsistent behavior of the alcoholic parent and the lack of support from the nonalcoholic parent
3. Worrying about the fights and arguments between the parents
4. Being scared and upset at the violence or possibility of violence in their family
5. Being upset at the parents' inappropriate behavior, which can include criminal or sexual behavior
6. Being disappointed by broken promises and feeling unloved
7. Feeling responsible for their parents' drinking

Many years ago, Margaret Cork, a social worker and pioneer in working with children of alcoholics in Canada, reported that children of alcoholics were more troubled by the arguing and fighting between their parents than by the alcoholic's drinking (1969).

Not all alcoholic families are the same. As a matter of fact, not all members of any given alcoholic family will be affected in the same way. For example, if you have siblings, do they see your parents, the alcoholism and their childhood experiences the same way you do? Many adult daughters of alcoholics have siblings who will not admit to being adult children of an alcoholic. Although you may have much in common with other adult daughters, your childhood experiences in an alcoholic family may have affected you differently. Some of the reasons for the differences are discussed below.

Your Age

Daughters who were born into an alcoholic family may have totally different perceptions and experiences than daughters whose parent(s) became alcoholic when they were fourteen. The younger you were when your parent became alcoholic, the longer you were exposed to active alcoholism and the higher the probability that you were negatively affected.

Additionally, your developmental stage of childhood might have influenced how you perceived alcoholism. For example, a five-year-old sees only the behavioral effects of alcoholism, which she equates with drunken behavior. A fifteen-year-old can equate alcoholism not only with being drunk, but also with a variety of perceived motivations as to why the alcoholic drinks.

Children do not automatically recognize that a parent is an alcoholic. As a matter of fact, many adult children will not accept even now that one or both of their parents is or was an alcoholic. In childhood, recognizing that the parent has a drinking problem occurs in three stages. In the first stage, a child begins to realize that her house is different from that of her friends. However, just because families differ does not mean that something is wrong. During the second stage, the child begins to suspect that the differences between her home and other homes is something that should be covered up or denied because she doesn't want her friends to know. In the third stage, the child becomes aware of what the difference is, which is that her parent drinks too much. Most daughters of alcoholics reach the third stage around age thirteen (Ackerman, 1988), which does not mean that the daughter tells anyone, but rather that she admits to herself that she knows what the problem is in her house. After all, many adult daughters admit the alcoholism only as adults, long after their childhood has ended.

Other factors influence the age at which daughters reach stage three. The gender of the alcoholic parent and whether one or two alcoholic parents were present are both contributing factors. For example, most daughters of alcoholic fathers reach stage three when they are twelve years old. (Approximately 60 percent of the adult daughters in this study had an alcoholic father only.) Daughters of two alcoholic parents typically admit the drinking problems when they are approximately fourteen years old. Perhaps both parents did not become alcoholic at the same time, or if a daughter has two alcoholic parents, she did not have a nonalcoholic role model to compare her adults to. Therefore, realizing the inappropriate behaviors in one's parents may take longer because they were both doing the same thing and not until being exposed to other parental role models does a daughter begin to admit the differences. (Only 20 percent of the adult daughters studied had two alcoholic parents.)

Daughters of alcoholic mothers often do not reach stage three until they are almost nineteen, perhaps because women traditionally have developed alcohol problems at later ages than men, or the daughter wants to deny a drinking problem longer in her mother than in her father. Another reason could be that adult daughters of alcoholic mothers are much less likely to know someone else with an alcoholic mother since only 20 percent of adult daughters have an alcoholic mother only, as opposed to the 60 percent who have an alcoholic father.

Alcoholic Mothers, Alcoholic Fathers

Are daughters of alcoholic mothers affected differently than daughters of alcoholic fathers? You may have entirely different memories, perceptions and experiences of your childhood depending upon the gender of your alcoholic parent. Additionally, if you had two alcoholic parents, the effects of the alcoholism of each one were probably not equally received; that is, you probably identified more with and were influenced more by the alcoholism in one parent than in the other, and experienced more positive or negative feelings from one than from the other. The impact and feelings of adult daughters of alcoholic mothers and fathers are discussed more fully in later chapters.

Contributing Others

While you were growing up, did you have someone special whom you could share your feelings with about your family life? Perhaps the person was another relative, a best friend, teacher, neighbor or, in some cases, your nonalcoholic parent. If you had someone who cared about you and your problems, she or he made a contribution to your life by helping you with your feelings. This special person allowed you to share your family secret. You may not have solved anything together, but just being together with another person and believing that someone else cared about you and supported you was helpful.

Unfortunately, only 13 percent of adult daughters indicate that they had someone with whom they could share their feelings during their childhood. Those daughters who did have such a person in their lives were much less likely to seek treatment as adults than those who had no choice but to keep all of their emotions and feelings to themselves. If you had such a friend, relative or confidante, as you proceed in your recovery from your childhood, you will realize how much she or he contributed to your life.

I wish I could have had real parents. I've always wondered what it would have been like to have someone to care about me and to share my deepest hurts and secrets and successes with.

Nancy

Parenting Behaviors and Styles

Although one or both of your parents were alcoholic while you were growing up, what kind of parent or parents were they? For example, how did the alcoholism affect the ability of the alcoholic to fulfill the parenting role? On the other hand, how did the alcoholism in the family affect the ability of your nonalcoholic parent to fulfill the parenting role?

Many adult daughters express that their strongest negative feelings about their childhood are more associated with how the alcoholic behaved toward them than with the actual drinking. In other words, the parenting that you received or didn't receive can affect your memories about your childhood more significantly than the drinking alone. How much the alcoholic parent attempts to still try and be a parent can affect a child. You may have had a parent who made an effort to be an effective parent, but who was unable to break the addiction from alcohol. Not all parents, alcoholic or nonalcoholic, have the same behaviors or the same styles of parenting. Growing up with a parent who ignores you is different than living with one who tries to control you, regardless of their alcohol use.

We felt that our father really did love us; he just wasn't very good at it. He messed up everything he tried, but he did try.

Carol

Other daughters were convinced that their alcoholic parent would lie awake at night trying to think of what else they could do to upset their daughter!

And when our father used to get us up in the middle of the night and march around the house singing "Onward Christian Soldiers," it would be a school night and we would think that we should be able to sleep like normal kids. And we'd say, "Mom, please help us, come to our rescue," and she never did.

Cathy

Adult daughters indicate that the behavior that they remember most about their alcoholic parent is the verbal belligerence. This type of alcoholic parent is argumentative and verbally abusive, walking all over everyone's beliefs and self-esteem.

Other daughters state that the alcoholic parent was offensive to them, including behaviors ranging from embarrassing them in front of friends, to physically or sexually abusing them. Thirty-one percent of adult daughters experienced physical abuse as children, 19 percent were victims of sexual abuse, and 38 percent witnessed spousal abuse in their families. These rates of abuse were three to four times higher than among women who were raised in nonalcoholic families. Daughters who experienced not only parental alcoholism but also abuse were affected more and differently than adult daughters of nonabusive alcoholics.

In my own recovery, I found that I slowly experienced and found ways to express anger at Dad for his various abusive rampages while he was drunk. The surprise was that I had seen my mother as a victim all those years and never held her responsible for the hell my brothers and I went through.

Valerie

Some adult daughters indicate that the alcoholic parent was passive and paid little attention to them or other members of the family. Other adult daughters state that the alcoholic pretended to be carefree, taking nothing seriously. This approach might have been fine according to the alcoholic's thinking, but adult daughters adjusted to this pattern by taking everything in their lives seriously, perhaps too seriously.

As you might suspect, verbal belligerence and offensive behaviors occur more among alcoholic parents than did passive and carefree behaviors. Additionally, daughters who experienced verbal attacks and abuse indicate far more negative effects than do the daughters of passive and carefree alcoholic parents.

Your Perceptions

Eighty percent of adult daughters perceive that having an alcoholic parent highly affected their lives. Twelve percent indicate that they were moderately affected, and 8 percent believe that they were unaffected. What is the source of their perceptions? Are their perceptions the ones that they had as children, or do they come from their experiences as adult daughters who see things differently now?

Your understanding of your childhood as a child may be totally different from how you remember it now. Whatever most of us define as real, we usually react to as if it exists. Whether it is real or not, we respond to it based on our perceptions. All daughters of alcoholics do not share the same perceptions of their experiences. This section began by asking what it was like in your home as a child. What did you *think* about your family as a child? Did you perceive and believe not only that something was wrong in your family, but also that you were being affected? If you thought that something was wrong, did you know what it was or did you think it was you?

When I was growing up I just felt very lonely all of the time. I felt like I didn't have any friends, that life was passing me by, and I was depressed often. I can't say that at the time I was experiencing it, I recognized it as being unnatural. You know I thought there was something wrong with me.

Paula

Having an accurate and consistent perception of a situation is difficult when the situation is chaotic and constantly changing, when it contains mixed messages, or when we are not able to understand what is happening. Many adult daughters admit to being confused as children not only about the drinking, but also about how they should behave in their own families.

For example, if you wanted to perceive that your parent did not have a drinking problem, then you would have tried to behave as if your mother was not alcoholic. However, this attempt became confusing when you found yourself doing things to compensate or cover up for a condition that you wanted to perceive did not exist.

Our perceptions of having an alcoholic parent can depend upon several things. The first and foremost is denial. While growing up, if you wanted to deny that your parent was alcoholic, you probably also denied that any problems from drinking existed. On the other hand, you could deny the impact of the drinking by convincing yourself that any dysfunctional behaviors in your family had nothing to do with drinking.

Another way to distort perceptions is to minimize. Such statements as "It really wasn't that bad," "It didn't affect me," or "He isn't drunk, he just doesn't feel well," are all examples of attempting to minimize the impact of the alcoholism in your life.

As a child, how well did you understand what was going

on in your family? In other words, did you know that alcoholism or alcohol problems were causing the pain in your family? If you did not fully understand what was happening, you probably do not accurately perceive the situation. As a child, your uncertainty about the situation could explain differences in opinions about what occurred.

All of these different perceptions and their reasons can explain why many adult daughters admit that they recognized the alcoholism in a parent as a child or teenager, while other adult daughters indicate that they did not perceive the problem of alcoholism until they were adults.

> My mother was an alcoholic, and I didn't know that she was an alcoholic when I was a child. So for me, being a child of an alcoholic didn't start until I was about fifteen years old. Before that, the experience was more of being a child in a family that was unloved and that I was a troublemaker and not wanted. Because of that, I felt I was to blame when I did find out that my mother was an alcoholic.
>
> *Renee*

Your Resiliency

A frequently heard cliché is that "children are resilient." Although this idea has been around for a long time, only in the past twenty years have therapists and researchers explored the validity of this concept. Much of this interest has come from our concern about "high-risk" children. Children who have been raised in troubled families—alcoholic, abusive, emotionally stressful, parents in conflict—or in dangerous physical environments have often been considered at-risk emotionally, physically and developmentally for many problems in their own lives. Certainly daughters of alcoholics fit this category.

On the other hand, some adult daughters were able to go with the flow as children and adolescents. They seemed to be able to adjust to situations, maintain a sense of purpose in their lives and, above all, keep a positive attitude. Parental alcoholism was not going to rain on their parade; the umbrella that protected them was resiliency.

Many definitions are available for resiliency, which can be described as the ability to thrive despite adversity. Resiliency enables people of all ages and backgrounds to lead healthy and fulfilling lives despite formidable obstacles. Different behavioral and emotional outcomes for many adult daughters might result from the amount of resiliency developed during childhood.

For example, while you were growing up, did you have people or institutions in your life that helped you? Did you have places to go that allowed you to feel good about yourself or at least forget about what was happening at home? Avis Brenner believes that all children under stress need an "emotional oasis" (1984). The child under stress needs a time-out somewhere from the trauma. Fortunately, some adult daughters had these places to go to and positive people in their lives.

Many studies on resiliency reveal that certain protective factors occur in the lives of high-risk children that help them successfully cope with their situations (Benard et al., 1994; Garmezy et al., 1976; Werner and Johnson, 2000). Children who have these protective factors are more able to endure the dysfunctional situations in their lives and still emerge as relatively competent and content children. The following are the six most common protective factors identified in the lives of resilient children.

1. **They know how to attract and use the support of adults.**

If you had people in your life helping and supporting you, perhaps not only did others want to help you, but you were also the type of girl that others enjoyed being around. Teachers, group leaders and adult relatives were there for you, and you were able to accept and use their support. Many adult daughters state that were it not for a certain adult or group of people in their lives, they would not have made it.

2. **They actively try to master their own environment, have a sense of their own power and often volunteer to help others.**

Few children can master the environment of an alcoholic family. However, children of alcoholics who could master other environments in their lives lessened the impact of their alcoholic families. For example, these children were able to fit in well in school and church, with youth groups and with friends. When you master your environment you feel comfortable in it—that you have something to contribute and that being in that environment is worthwhile. Most importantly, you feel good about yourself. Daughters of alcoholics who mastered an environment had a place not only to feel good about themselves, but also to enjoy an emotional oasis from their families.

3. **They develop a high degree of autonomy early in life.**

You cannot totally separate from an alcoholic family. However, those daughters of alcoholics who were able to establish an identity other than being a daughter of an alcoholic were able to develop a certain degree of autonomy. I used to call this "the front-porch phenomenon." Whenever I was inside my house, I would shut down. In the grip of too much tension and too much dysfunction, you become part of a dysfunctional system even if you don't want to. Being a spectator was not possible. I was enmeshed whether I liked it or not. When I left the house, however, and stepped off the front porch, I felt a tremendous sense of relief and I believed that for a while I could be my own person. How about you? Did you have a chance to separate for a while, or did being a member of an alcoholic family totally overshadow your identity?

4. **They become involved in various activities or projects and do well in most things that they undertake.**

A little bit of success somewhere provides a wonderful way to offset a lot of pain in your family. Daughters of alcoholics today have more opportunities to become involved in activities than many of the adult daughters who were part of the original study on which this book is based. Adult daughters often share that they felt like failures at home or were put down by the alcoholic. The actress Suzanne Somers, a daughter of an alcoholic, publicly tells her story and states that she was constantly called a "zero, the big 'O,' or nothing" by her alcoholic father, which must have been incredibly painful.

Daughters who were involved in various activities and did well in them had a chance to experience successes in their lives. These daughters, even in pain, were able to use their talents and feel good about themselves. One woman in the play A Chorus Line tells of the pain in her family and the marital infidelity of her father, who left the family, but she states that, "Everything was beautiful at the ballet." For a few hours a week, she danced there and the world danced with her.

5. **They are socially at ease, and they make others feel comfortable around them.**

I think that I have done a lot for children. I have developed programs for high-risk children, worked with youth mental-health workers, helped to found organizations to advocate for children's issues and listened to thousands of children. I would, however, be the last person to say that I love all children. You could put some children around me for a long time and I don't think that the word "love" would come up between the two of us too often. Some children are easier to help than others.

When they are comfortable in social situations and others feel comfortable around them, children are more likely to benefit from help. Whether the person who is going to help realizes it or not, if she is comfortable around the child she will give the child everything she has. If, however, something about the child makes her uncomfortable, she is likely to be hesitant or cautious even if she is not aware that she is doing it.

Many adult daughters have great social skills. They know the right things to do around other people and thus others are at ease in their presence. If these adult daughters possessed these traits as girls, they probably had more people who were willing to interact with them and thus be supportive. Daughters who have always struggled socially may not have been as fortunate.

6. **They develop a healthy sense of humor.**

Traditionally we have always thought that having a healthy sense of humor around stress was an adult characteristic. We now realize, however, that children who have a healthy sense of humor are more resilient to stress. I'm not talking about being sarcastic. Being sarcastic about your situation is much different from having a healthy sense of humor.

Sarcasm does not indicate that you have the ability to deflect or reduce the emotional impact of strain. If anything, sarcasm might be an indicator of just how much the pain exists. I've listened to many adult daughters who made joke after joke or wisecracks about their alcoholic family, but you could feel the pain.

A healthy sense of humor does not mean that you could laugh at everything as much as it might have indicated that you were able to have an alternative point of view about the situation. Also, a healthy sense of humor as a child meant that sometimes you knew that the best thing to do was to just "lighten up." You knew that you couldn't change the situation, but maybe you could make it less intense. G. K. Chesterton, a British philosopher, once said that the reason that angels can fly is because they take themselves lightly.

Did you have any of the above contributors to resiliency while you were growing up? Such personality characteristics might help to explain differences among adult daughters. Looking at the resiliency factors might remind you not only of your childhood, but also your experiences outside of your family. Sometimes we need to look back to see who helped us, and sometimes we are able to remember good people and positive situations. Now you need to find more of those.

AFTERTHOUGHTS

Whoever inquires about our childhood
wants to know something about our soul.

ERIKA BURKHART

I think my father and the rest of them invented the happy family
and put it into movies to drive everyone crazy.

JILL ROBINSON

Before a secret is told, one can often feel
the weight of it in the atmosphere.

SUSAN GRIFFIN

One form of loneliness is to have a memory
and no one to share it with.

PHYLLIS ROSE

Memories are the key not to the past, but to the future.

CORRIE TEN BOOM

Chapter 3

What Did You Learn at Home Today?

What did you learn during your childhood? I am not talking about what you learned in school, but rather what you learned about yourself and especially what you learned from your family. Whether you were aware of it or not, the lessons that you learned from your family affected you not only during your childhood, but many of these early lessons also remain with you today. In fact, according to the Keri Report on Confidence and the American Woman, approximately 40 percent of women state that their self-confidence was a result of their upbringing (1988). Your family-influenced childhood lessons have affected many of your values and opinions about relationships, intimacy, parenting skills and career choices, and most importantly your self-esteem.

As the daughter of an alcoholic, during your childhood you were learning three things simultaneously, two of which are common to the experiences of daughters from nonalcoholic families. You were learning how to grow as a child and a human being. The second was learning to be a girl and a young woman. Finally, you learned how to adjust to belonging to an alcoholic family.

Learning to become a child and a human being are referred to as normal developmental tasks. Many theorists, including Erik Erikson, believe that humans progress through stages in their lives, and at each stage the person is confronted with a particular task (Erikson, 1963). Gail Sheehy, in her book *Passages*, writes that we all go through different periods or passages in our lives, and each period has its unique emotions, characteristics and challenges (1978).

According to Erikson's theories, the tasks involved in our lives occur in eight different stages. At every stage, we are faced with trying to resolve a particular conflict. If we are successful, we achieve conflict resolution. As a child, if you were not able to adequately work through a given stage or conflict, your task would remain unresolved into adulthood.

Before we discuss each stage and its particular task, an important part of this theory to remember is that how well we do at one stage determines not only how well we have handled the task, but also how successfully we will complete the next stage of our lives. Each stage thus becomes a prerequisite for the next.

Adult daughters often state that they feel as if the sequence of the stages did not occur properly. Many adult daughters share that they were forced to grow up too quickly or that they never experienced the emotions of childhood. Although this book is written to and about *adult* daughters, much of who you are, what you believe and how you feel developed during your childhood stage. If the period of childhood did not influence us as adults, we would not need adult children's programs! While we may wish that childhood memories ended with childhood, life doesn't work that way. When childhood is over, the leftovers are called adults. Think of how nice your childhood could have been had you been able to tell your family, "I am a child, and until all of my developmental and emotional needs are appropriately met, I will not be going on to adolescence!"

The eight stages of development fall into periods of childhood, adolescence and adulthood. At each stage, people are looking for a positive resolution to a normal conflict. Without that resolution, negative results occur.

Childhood Tasks

Trust Versus Mistrust

The development of trust in our lives is the first task and, according to Erikson, is the most critical of all of the stages. Developing trust provides the foundation upon which the successful resolutions of all other tasks depend. For young children who are not able to develop a healthy sense of trust in themselves and in others, Erikson believed that the opposite would develop and that they would become mistrusting. To develop trust in childhood, young children of alcoholics, as well as all children, need to be exposed to trustworthy adults.

How much trust existed in your alcoholic family? Was the amount of trust related to the amount of drinking? Was the situation in your family that the more people were drinking, the less anyone trusted each other? More importantly, can you trust people today? Adult children are often said to be "either-or" in giving their trust. Either we refuse to trust anyone, or we give our trust too easily, which usually results in pain.

One of the most difficult forms of trust to learn as adult children is whether we can trust others with information about ourselves. This form of trust is scary and involves risk because we trust that at a later time in our relationship the other person will not use what we have shared with them against us or to harm us. In most alcoholic families, the rule about sharing information was *keep it to yourself.*

> I didn't know what trust was. Every time I got involved in trusting at home, or trusting that my mom wasn't going to drink, or she was going to work her program, I was devastated when she didn't. So that just blew trust right out the window for me.
>
> *Veleta*

Autonomy Versus Shame and Doubt

Children need to learn that they can do things for themselves and not be overly controlled. At the same time, they need consistent guidance to be able to learn. If healthy balance between autonomy and belonging does not occur, a self-concept of inadequacy and shame develops.

Here comes that famous word known by every adult child: *control*. In most alcoholic families, everyone is trying to maintain some control over an uncontrollable situation. For example, your father is trying to control his drinking, your mother is trying to control your father and (if you were a "good" child) you were trying to control both of them. Children in alcoholic families are overly controlled. Either others are attempting to control children too much, or children are trying to control the family too much. You were probably not given the opportunity to develop a healthy sense of self-control. Without developing self-control, shame develops and doubt about our abilities to exercise control over our lives begins to occur.

> Control for me goes hand-in-hand with the fear of abandonment. When I was sixteen years old I had almost complete responsibility over my brothers and sisters, and I didn't think anything of it. I thought it was perfectly normal to come home from school, go to the babysitter's and pick up my siblings, feed them, clean house, put them to bed, wash their clothes and all that. It didn't seem to me to be abnormal, but I think my control issue started at sixteen because everything was so bizarre. Everything was out of control. I would walk into the house and never know what to expect. Was it going to be war? Was it going to be a carnival? I never knew. And I ran off and got married. I found somebody who was very needy and I married him. I was in control, sixteen years old, and I had complete control.
>
> *Audrey*

Do you ever feel like your life is out of control or that others control you against your will? Ironically, we often react to the lack of control by attempting to control others. Besides, we often believe that one of the best ways to make sense of chaos is to take charge. Who was in charge of your family while you were growing up? Was control equally or reasonably shared? More importantly, were you allowed your fair share of control in order to develop a healthy sense of autonomy?

Initiative Versus Guilt

Conflicts between your initiative and guilt feelings may have begun when adults treated your curiosity about the world as inappropriate. If your questions were ignored or hushed up and your normal childhood games were restricted, you likely developed many guilty feelings without knowing the cause. In order for you to develop a healthy sense of initiative, your parents needed to maintain a balance between the rules and the amount of permission that you were given for your behaviors. Parental consistency is the key to achieving a proper sense of initiative. Erikson believed that inconsistency did more harm than being too restrictive.

How did you handle the inconsistency in your house? Many adult daughters reacted by becoming overly conforming or people-pleasing, often resulting in subjugation of normal childhood activities. Another common pattern at this stage is for the child to imitate the behavior that she observes in the adults around her. Needless to say, this method of coping lays the foundation for repeating the behaviors of inappropriate adult role models.

What makes you feel guilty today? If being yourself makes you feel guilty, you may have given up your normal childhood curiosity in exchange for inappropriate feelings about yourself. If you feel guilty unless you put everyone else first, you have sacrificed your normal interests and growth. Worse is feeling guilty for actions and people over which you have absolutely no control, but somehow you think are your responsibility.

Industry Versus Inferiority

Always feeling inferior puts you at a disadvantage in every relationship you have.

Robyn

During this stage of our childhood, we need to develop a feeling of usefulness. Unfortunately, in many alcoholic homes children begin to believe that they are useless or that their accomplishments are always second to the drinking problems. For children to accomplish this developmental task, parents must express interest in the child's accomplishments. Merely doing most of the work in the house does not contribute to a personal sense of usefulness for children. Rather, the act of doing housework outside of any larger context contributes to a sense of being used, or of being valued only for what you do, not for who you are. In the face of repeated rejection, children begin to feel unlovable. Repeatedly being rejected equals lost self-esteem.

You know, I had ways of getting attention, but it never seemed to be enough. I still had this sense of being alone. I remember a lot of times trying to get my dad's attention. I don't know if that was unnatural or what, but I remember thinking in grade school if I would just go to school and get hit by a car, someone would pay attention to me. You know, feeling like I would just die and then everybody would pay attention to me.

Ada

Adolescence Tasks

Identity Versus Diffusion

Remember your "reputation" in high school? Some of us would like to forget it. No one is more conscious of identity than a teenager, especially because of wanting to fit in and the desire to find a place to belong. The development of identity neither begins nor ends in adolescence, but begins to solidify during adolescence.

Growing through this process with all of the confusion of adolescence is difficult enough, let alone trying to accomplish it in the midst of mixed family messages and confusion. One's negative family identity begins to overshadow the developing sense of personal identity. When this stage of our lives begins and we carry many unresolved issues from our childhood stages, the tasks of adolescence become even more difficult.

> I was always ridiculed as a child and I always gave my power away to other people, to other kids. Whatever they said to me, I felt they were stronger, they were more important than I was, so whatever was said about me I believed. I just isolated myself and just pretended like I was a tough little girl who didn't need anyone. And I'm still doing it.
>
> *Barbara*

Intimacy Versus Isolation

Developing the skills necessary to establish positive emotional intimacy is the most critical developmental task for children of alcoholics. Intimacy problems begin when people push you away and reject you. The core of all intimacy problems is a fear that other people will abandon you.

If you were successful at this stage, you emerged with a healthy sense of self-love and the abilities to like and genuinely love others. If this skill and emotional closeness did not develop, you probably became emotionally isolated from your own feelings and from people around you.

Another risk at this stage occurs when you confuse

intimacy with something else. For example, constantly giving too much to others in hopes of receiving something in return is not being intimate, especially when you receive nothing in return, but keep trying because you feel that you are to blame for the lack of intimacy. This type of relationship is not intimacy but is instead allowing others to misuse you. Robin Norwood points this problem out repeatedly in her book *Women Who Love Too Much* (1985).

> I never remember being hugged as a child. I never remember being told that they loved me, or I was loveable. So I never felt those things.
>
> *Sue*

Adult Tasks

Although these tasks are not from childhood, we will include them since our childhood obviously and significantly affected how well we can work through our adult tasks.

Generativity Versus Self-Absorption

Generativity, which is the basis of our parenting skills, is the ability to give beyond us to the next generation. To be effective parents, all of the previous skills should be learned correctly. However, we know that one of the most frequently mentioned problems of adult daughters relates to the concern about their ability to be healthy parents. A tremendous amount of our attitudes and values as parents come from our childhoods and particularly from the role models that we observed.

My biggest fear is that I will hurt my children. . . . . I will repeat
or have been repeating the very same types of behaviors, which I
felt hurt me, that my parents displayed.

Gayle

Integrity Versus Disgust

Integrity means that we are accepting responsibility for
our own lives and that we do not blame others; that we have
learned to like who we are and what we believe; and that we
have developed healthy self-concepts about ourselves. I see
integrity as synonymous with Abraham Maslow's concept of
self-actualization, whereby we truly become and live as we
wish to be (1968).

Do you like yourself? Do you love yourself? Unfortunately,
the most negative legacy of alcoholic families is producing
adults who do not like themselves. I would argue that living
with yourself, if you do not like who you are, is far more difficult than living with an alcoholic parent!

Often we tolerate harmful behaviors in others for a long
time. However, when we do things that we do not like or
want to do, we can't stand it. We can emerge from negative
experiences not liking ourselves very much, which creates a
great dilemma for most of us. We would like to have healthy
relationships with others, but what do we do when we don't
like what we are offering them—ourselves?

The core of recovery is related to this last stage. By working through all of the previous stages and becoming the kind
of people that we would like to be, we can recover from
alcoholism, from missing certain developmental stages and
from us. We gain the ability to look in the mirror and like
what we see.

As you read through these developmental stages, did anything become obvious to you about yourself or about adult

children? Let us again consider the characteristics that supposedly result from unresolved developmental tasks. Lack of trust, shame and doubt, guilt, feeling inferior, identity confusion, isolation, lack of parenting skills, and not becoming the kind of person that you would like to be are all results of unsuccessful conflict resolution.

Where have you heard these characteristics before? Aren't these characteristics some of the same ones that adult children so often mention? Could it be that not having a healthy childhood contributed to these problems for adult children? Well, the answer is obvious, isn't it? Yet, too often we look only at the alcohol or the drinking to explain problems for adult children, and not at the childhood experiences themselves and how they have contributed positively and negatively to your growth.

Even in light of certain differences, children of alcoholics have plenty in common with all other children. They all have common childhood experiences and developmental tasks. Although life might seem otherwise at the time, alcoholism in the family typically does not totally dictate and put limits on life. Adult daughters of alcoholics have more in common with all women than differences. Yet these adult daughters also know pain that other women do not. They know pain that has deep roots, which was planted in childhood.

After a While

*After a while you learn
the subtle difference between
holding a hand and chaining a soul
and you learn
that love doesn't mean leaning
and company doesn't mean security.
And you begin to learn
that kisses aren't contracts
and presents aren't promises
and you begin to accept your defeats
with your head up and your eyes ahead
with the grace of a woman, not the grief of a child
and you learn
to build all your roads on today
because tomorrow's ground is
too uncertain for plans
and futures have a way of falling down
in mid-flight.
After a while you learn
that even sunshine burns
if you get too much
so you plant your own garden
and decorate your own soul
instead of waiting for someone
to bring you flowers.
And you learn that you really can endure
you really are strong
you really do have worth
and you learn
and you learn
with every good-bye, you learn . . .*

©1971 Veronica A. Shoffstall

AFTERTHOUGHTS

Words are more powerful than perhaps anyone suspects,
and once deeply engraved in a child's mind,
they are not easily eradicated.

MAY SARTON

A story is told as much by silence as by speech.

SUSAN GRIFFIN

Feel the fear, and do it anyway.

SUSAN JEFFERS

It occurred to me when I was thirteen and wearing white gloves
and Mary Janes and going to dancing school
that no one should have to dance backward all their lives.

JILL RUCKELSHAUS

Nothing is really lost. It's just where it doesn't belong.

SUZANNE MUELLER

Chapter 4

These Are the
Things I Learned

She was never there for me because she was either drunk or drugged. I saw things as a little girl I should never have seen or done because of my mother and what I was forced to do.

Pat

What happened to you as a result of growing up in a crisis situation? The developmental problems discussed in the previous chapter are not the result of only one explanation, such as the failure to work through developmental tasks. They are a combination of many factors.

For example, in chapter 2, age was identified as one of the factors that explains why adult daughters are not all the same. One can speculate whether or not a particular problem for an adult daughter is related to not only her age when the alcoholism in the family developed, but also the developmental task she was trying to work through when the alcoholism began.

For instance, are adult daughters who have problems trusting others more likely to have been born into an alcoholic family, or to have had the alcoholism develop when they were very young and trying to establish trust, which was the first developmental task of their lives? Or are adult daughters who have intimacy problems more likely to have had a practicing alcoholic parent when they were teenagers and struggling to establish intimacy skills? Problems for daughters of alcoholics are a combination of living in an alcoholic family and their success or failure at working through normal developmental tasks.

Adjusting to Your Family

Lee Ann Hoff, in her book *People in Crisis,* believes that one of three results can occur within a person who lives through a crisis (1984). The first result is that the person in crisis attempts to reduce the anxiety and tension by developing patterns of negative behaviors. Many adult daughters indicate that they adjusted to their situation by engaging in behaviors—such as becoming isolated, withdrawn, overly controlling or people-pleasing—as a response to the alcoholism. At the same time, they were aware that their behaviors were not only ineffective in stopping the alcoholism, but also that such behaviors served to sacrifice their own health and emotional needs.

The second response to a crisis assumes that the person in a crisis can return to a precrisis state—that the individual would remain the same as before the crisis developed and that the crisis would have no lasting effects. Unfortunately, few adult daughters indicate they are able to return to a pre-alcoholic condition. One condition to make this result possible would be that the alcoholic would become sober. Unfortunately, most studies reveal that only about 10 percent of alcoholics get sober. Therefore, this precrisis state is not likely to occur, and your exposure to alcoholism will likely continue to have effects on you. Remember, only 8 percent of adult daughters indicate that the family's alcoholism did not affect them.

The third outcome of a crisis occurs when the person not only survives the crisis, but also emerges with behaviors and strengths that she would not have developed had she not lived through the crisis. Obviously, all three of the outcomes could occur for any adult daughter.

A combination of the first and the third responses seems to occur for the majority of adult daughters. Both positive and negative behaviors and emotions develop as a result of the exposure to the alcoholic parent. Most of the time, however, the negative effects begin to dominate, or you are so conditioned to focus on your negative behaviors that you seldom consider your assets. Obviously, any assets emerging from an alcoholic family were painfully learned.

Crisis equals danger, but it also equals opportunity. With intervention and recovery, the painful lessons of childhood can become the foundation of growth and strength as an adult.

For example, if you had no choice as a young girl but to take care of yourself because others couldn't, you now know that you *can* take care of yourself. As stated earlier, adult daughters, as well as all children of alcoholics, are survivors. In order to survive you have developed strengths. You may or may not be aware of them, or you may not have considered that many of your behaviors do have potential benefits. Ironically, sometimes we do things before we have "discovered" what we have done.

> Being an adult daughter is a very conflicting place to be, especially if you become aware of this later in life. On the one hand you feel you finally found out why you've been different all your life. You're also angry that so much has passed, but you're also happy that you've survived, made something of yourself and finally achieved "peace."
>
> *Toni*

Gender Identity

While you were handling the above tasks in your life, you were also developing your gender identity as a girl and young woman. Although we advocate role changes for both females and males in our culture, we are not attempting to abandon our concepts of femininity and masculinity. Rather than moving toward gender-role changes, we are probably attempting role convergence, which would occur when either gender can fulfill a role with an equal amount of competency and respect and still maintain gender identity.

Another point about gender socialization involves what happened to you as a child and what you expect from yourself today. For example, your childhood may have occurred during a period in our society when gender patterns were very distinct and you emerged with an unconscious set of female expectations. However, as an adult woman these patterns may no longer be applicable. If the patterns of your childhood and your adulthood are different, you face a dilemma between how you were raised and how you would like to live as a woman today. This same type of problem exists when you consider how you adjusted as a child to an alcoholic family and how you would like to live today as an adult. Your childhood behaviors may have carried over into your adulthood and kept you from growing. Unconsciously, you may still be reacting to others as if you were still living at home. Both of these situations—your gender socialization and adjusted childhood behaviors—can create many mixed messages that keep pulling you back unconsciously. These messages started in childhood, but what were they?

What happens to the gender development of young females in the alcoholic family? In our society, we have experienced "expressive" role socialization for women. Historically, this pattern has resulted in women developing emotionally expressive, nurturing, other-directed and supportive roles (Zelditch, 1955; Sanford and Donovan, 1985). Does exposure to an alcoholic parent alter this pattern?

Claudia Bepko, in her book *The Responsibility Trap*, believes that gender development in the alcoholic family is intensified. For example, rather than changing typical gender patterns for girls in the alcoholic family, the daughter is often expected to become even more understanding, more nurturing and more oriented to meeting others' needs than are daughters raised in nonalcoholic families. She states that "females learn that they must be nurturers who never ask for nurturing" and "women are socialized to be emotionally over-responsible. . . . Messages about appropriate adult dependency needs are contradicting and paradoxical— women are to be both dependent and primary emotional caretakers, but are never to express their own emotional needs" (1985). Certainly, clinical observations and the many stories that adult daughters share support this theory. Many adult daughters state that they became the expressive center of their family and that they felt that their responsibility was to ensure that all family matters were under control and emotionally satisfied.

> I constantly told everyone that everything was okay. It was not my father's fault, just give it to me and I'll take care of it.
>
> *Ruth*

A common pattern seems to emerge for many adult daughters. This pattern involves the intensifying of gender role identity to the point that meeting her personal needs becomes difficult. She is at risk in the alcoholic family of becoming a person who is out of balance because she is disproportionately expected to meet the needs of others, which causes problems for working through her particular developmental goals. Many of the very characteristics that she values as a female, such as her ability to identify emotionally and effectively with issues and people, can place her at risk of being used by others due to their inability to handle their own problems. Adult daughters consistently express their pain over being placed in a position of surrogate parent or spouse because of family alcoholism, when all they wanted to do was to have a "normal" childhood.

Perhaps you can identify with some of these positions in your own life. If you felt that you were responsible or you were to blame for most of the activities in your family, then you overly identified with your perception of your responsibilities. Lynn Sanford, coauthor of *Women & Self-Esteem*, believes that women, more than men, are more likely to hold themselves personally responsible when something goes wrong (1988). For example, Sanford believes that if something goes wrong for a male, he is more likely to look outside of himself first for the reason. He will look for *external* reasons for these problems. However, women are more likely to look *internally* or blame themselves first when things go wrong before they will blame others. Unfortunately, alcoholic families are breeding grounds for these types of patterns for daughters.

Childhood Lessons

Looking back on your life, how well have you handled your learning tasks of human development, adjusting to an alcoholic family and becoming a woman? Are you aware of how each area influenced the other? Are you aware of positive and negative lessons that were learned in childhood?

We may not always be aware of what we have learned. While lessons are being taught, we usually learn two things simultaneously. We learn the intended lessons, which are supposed to happen, and we learn the unintended lessons, which are unanticipated consequences of the learning process.

For example, as a child you learned to read. Someone spent time with you for the express purpose of teaching you to read. The fact that you have progressed this far in this book means that you succeeded in learning how to read. However, what did you learn about reading itself? Did you learn that you like to read, or did you learn that reading is something that you *must* do? Some children found learning to read an incredibly difficult and embarrassing process because they did not read as well as the other children. They eventually did learn to read, but additionally they learned that they hated reading.

Therefore, during your childhood you learned many intended and unintended lessons from your alcoholic family. Normal human development should include the intended lessons of your life, but many unintended lessons are also learned from living in an alcoholic family. These lessons can be painful and last a lifetime unless they can be unlearned or changed from childhood liabilities to adulthood assets.

Did you unintentionally learn any of the following lessons as a daughter in an alcoholic family?

- If I can control everything, I can keep my family from becoming upset.
- If I please everyone, everyone will be happy.
- Whatever happens is my fault, and I am to blame when trouble occurs.
- People who love you the most are those who cause you the most pain.
- If I don't get too close emotionally, you cannot hurt me.
- My responsibility is to ensure that everyone in the family gets along with each other.
- Take care of others first.
- Nothing is wrong, but I don't feel right.
- Expressing anger is not appropriate.
- Something is missing in my life.

- I'm unique, and my family is different from all other families.
- I can deny anything.
- I am not a good person.
- I am responsible for the success of a relationship.
- To be acceptable, everything must be perfect.

All of the above messages have one thing in common: negative consequences for your own growth and recovery as an adult daughter. These childhood lessons become imprints or beliefs that you have about yourself, and they begin to dictate your expectations of yourself and your behaviors. If you examine these lessons closely, you will see that living by these "rules" will lead to a life out of balance.

However, you have survived and somehow you have maintained some balance in your life. Therefore, you must have learned other lessons that have served you well or have allowed you to survive. Again, you may not be fully aware of these other lessons. As a matter of fact, for many adult daughters not only are these lessons unintended, but also in many cases, they are undiscovered. These lessons are the painfully positive lessons of your childhood. In other words, they can have positive results for you, but they have been learned as the result of experiencing pain.

Why are these painfully positive lessons undiscovered? Usually because when we are in the middle of a crisis, we do not have the time or the awareness to look for benefits. We are too busy surviving. An unspoken motto for many children of alcoholics might be, "Survive now and heal later."

While living in an alcoholic family, how many of us thought that anything positive was happening or that anything positive could possibly come from our experiences? While being raised in an alcoholic family is not necessarily a positive experience, Lee Ann Hoff's idea that some people come through a crisis and learn behaviors and strengths that they would not have developed otherwise has value (1984). If we develop any benefits from a crisis experience, we more likely become aware of them after the crisis is over. Therefore, as an adult daughter you are now in a position to determine whether you have learned anything from your negative childhood experiences that you could use to your benefit as an adult.

For example, many adult daughters who have learned the following lessons are in the process of discovering not only these lessons, but also the best parts of themselves.

Can you identify with any of these undiscovered qualities?

- I am a survivor. I can survive.
- I have developed competencies in many areas of my life.
- I can handle crises.
- I have a good sense of empathy.
- I can take care of myself.
- I am not easily discouraged.
- I can find alternatives to problems.
- I am not afraid to rely on my abilities.
- I can be healthy when others are not.
- I do have choices.
- People can depend on me.
- I appreciate my inner strength.
- I know what I want.
- I am a good person.
- I may not be perfect, but parts of me are great.

I have learned to be grateful for the experiences of my childhood. I know that I am a survivor and that I have incredible strengths that served me well. . . . I love me. I am excited about the future, and I am excited about TODAY.

Karen

To Be, or Not to Be, a Good COA

Another challenge in your childhood years might have been trying to make a choice between two options: You could either adapt to the alcoholism and try to become a "good" child of an alcoholic, or you could try to have a normal childhood and have your developmental needs met. Unfortunately, doing both was difficult.

If you were a good child of an alcoholic (COA), then you would have engaged in many of the behaviors that led to developing the negative lessons shown on page 78. To be a good COA, you were called upon to deny the alcoholism and other family problems, subjugate your developmental needs, hide your emotions, please others, pretend you were happy and be a "perfect daughter." Those behaviors do not produce happy childhoods, let alone healthy adults.

On the other hand, trying to have a "normal" childhood probably didn't work out either. To have a healthy childhood, you needed others around you to be able to successfully fill their support roles. Most members of an alcoholic family are so emotionally drained that they are unable to meet a child's needs on a consistent basis.

Therefore, if you tried to become the perfect daughter, you were denied your own needs. If you tried to develop and have the same experiences as children from nonalcoholic families, you quickly discovered that you were severely limited in your attempts to be normal. Either way, the outcomes were painful. However, if you were like most adult daughters, you probably tried to do both. Obviously, some adult daughters were able to do some of each more successfully than others. Regardless of how successfully you played both roles, you felt pain, denial of emotions and the sense that your life was out of control. These two lessons of childhood, like all of your other lessons, are somewhere inside of you today.

Your Childhood Spirit

Erikson tells us that the greatest crime of humanity is to destroy the spirit of a child (1963). Inside all of us is a childhood spirit. For some adult daughters, this spirit has been neglected, abused and bruised, but it has managed to endure. Other adult daughters are aware that the spirit is emerging from the clouds of childhood, dusting itself off and stating to the world that "I am alive." This spirit of childhood is that part of all of us that wants to experience and enjoy life to the greatest of our potential. The childhood spirit constantly reminds us to take risks, feel emotions, reach out for warmth and communicate with the inner parts of ourselves that have been silenced too long. The childhood spirit tells you that you will not have this day again, to use this day for all it is worth—that life is not a rehearsal.

If you are not in touch with your childhood spirit as an adult, your spirit has probably been neglected or denied and more importantly is currently not available for your recovery. What could cause your spirit to be absent? Typically, we look for the cause by asking, "What happened to you as a child?" We are looking for the ways in which you were victimized. Certainly, adult children were the victims of many factors and events during their childhoods. However, the greatest pain for many adult children may not be what happened to them as children, especially if they were not aware of the many forms of victimization that occurred. The greatest emotional pain for adult children occurs not when they realize that they have been victimized, but rather when they become aware of what they have missed.

What Did You Miss as a Child?

If your parents were withdrawn, you missed being nurtured. If your family was violent, you missed living without fear. If your father ridiculed you, you missed acceptance. If all of the energy in your family centered on the alcoholic, you missed feeling loved.

In conducting research for this book, at the end of each interview I would ask the same question of the adult daughters of alcoholics, "Is there anything that you would like to add?" I was surprised at how many times I heard the same answer no matter where I was conducting interviews. I began to think that all adult daughters knew each other!

In response to my question, I often heard, "I'm okay now, I'm doing better, really. But I don't know. . . . Sometimes I just feel as if there is something missing." After about five hundred adult daughters told me something was missing, I finally figured out the reason they told me that: Something *was* missing in their lives! They all had an empty feeling that somehow life should offer more or they should be "getting more out of life."

For the adult daughters, many different things were missing: childhood spirits, a sense of contentment, intimacy in relationships or feeling good about themselves. Some adult daughters felt the painful awareness of missing a nurturing family while they were young and realizing that the past cannot be changed.

Something is absent. You can feel it, but not find it. These "missing moments" in life occur when you see things in others that remind you of what you don't have. For example, you pass a romantic couple on the street. Whether they are both sixteen or eighty years old doesn't matter. You can tell that they have a quality relationship and you feel good for them. However, if your relationship is in shambles or you have never had a great relationship, the quality of theirs will remind you of what is missing in yours.

Discovering what is missing and how to find or restore it is part of recovery. Learning to discover what you missed in childhood is also a lesson from childhood. However, seeing what you missed as a child is easier now that you are an adult.

If you can pull lessons from all of the topics we discussed in this chapter, you can learn and discover that your childhood spirit is alive and well, hiding in your adult body. Yes, the period of childhood is over, but the spirit of childhood is still available today. You have learned many lessons, survived much pain and developed many skills. The true lessons of our past lie not only in what we have learned, but also what we have remembered that can help us grow today.

> Most of what I really need to know about how to live and what to do and how to be, I learned in kindergarten. Wisdom was not at the top of the graduate school mountain, but there in the sandbox at nursery school.
>
> These are the things I learned: Share everything. Play fair. Don't hit people. Put things back where you found them. Clean up your own mess. Don't take things that aren't yours. Say you're sorry when you hurt somebody. . . . Learn some and think some and draw and paint and sing and dance and play and work every day some. . . .
>
> When you go out into the world, watch for traffic, hold hands and stick together. Be aware of wonder. . . .
>
> Think of what a better world it would be if we all—the whole world—had cookies and milk about three o'clock every afternoon and then lay down with our blankets for a nap. Or if we had a basic policy in our nation and other nations to always put things back where we found them and cleaned up our own messes. And it is still true, no matter how old you are, when you go out into the world, it is best to hold hands and stick together.
>
> *Robert Fulghum*

AFTERTHOUGHTS

The events of childhood do not pass,
but repeat themselves like seasons of the year.

ELEANOR FARJEON

The best mind-altering drug is truth.

LILY TOMLIN

I'm not frightened of the darkness outside.
It's the darkness inside houses I don't like.

SHELAGH DELANEY

I know I'm a bridge between two worlds.
All I ask is for people to wash their feet
before they try to walk on me.

ALANIS OBAMSAWIN

Invisibility is not a natural state for anyone.

MITSUYE YAMADA

Part Two

Collecting

Emotional Baggage

Chapter 5

Alcoholic Mothers: Pains of Endearment*

*All of the quotes in this chapter are from adult daughters of alcoholic mothers.

As a child it seemed like my mother was almost always angry, or extremely loving. I never knew when I came home which it would be. Either she might be warm and loving, or she might be cold and hostile. It was scary to live in a house like that. You were out of control. You never knew what to expect. I got to the point where I would isolate myself and try to make myself invisible if I knew I wasn't doing something that would be approved of, or something that I would be accepted for. . . . She didn't really spend a lot of time with me or share a lot of her life with me. I never really knew why. I thought it was me.

Miriam

Adult daughters of alcoholic mothers indicated that having an alcoholic mother taught them a variety of often confusing and painful lessons. Most adult daughters with alcoholic mothers described their growing-up experiences as filled with anger, disgust and disappointment, and devoid of bonding and nurturing. Adult daughters of alcoholic mothers were more "attacking" in their comments than were daughters of alcoholic fathers.

On the other hand, a few adult daughters of alcoholic mothers wanted to deny even more emphatically that their mothers were alcoholics and wanted to protect them. These adult daughters did not want to accept that their mothers could be alcoholics and tried to remain close to them despite the drinking.

Please tell me that just because my mom was an alcoholic that she was not a "bad" person. She was always there for me and did everything and more that a mother is supposed to do.

Janine

Adult daughters of alcoholic mothers, therefore, shared a variety of childhood lessons based on whether or not the daughters were angry with their mothers or tried to protect them. Either way, adult daughters of alcoholic mothers learned some of the following lessons:

- I am angry with my mother.
- I wanted to love my mother, but she and her behavior kept pushing me away.
- I learned to be disappointed and disgusted with my mother, and I have difficulty respecting her.
- I learned how to be responsible for my mother's duties, and I resented always being in charge.
- I was denied information about my own sexual identity, how to be a woman and how to prepare for my future roles.
- I was taught unhealthy ways to relate to other people.
- I experienced poor parenting skills, and I am unsure of my own parenting skills.
- I find it difficult to trust other women.
- I felt abandoned and let down.
- I am not sure of how to give and receive nurturing, because I was not nurtured.

If you had an alcoholic mother, chances are you felt even more isolated than did adult daughters of alcoholic fathers. If your mother was an alcoholic, you likely have different issues than do daughters of alcoholic fathers.

Did you ever feel that at least daughters with alcoholic fathers can find other daughters to talk to about their problems? Statistically, we know that only one out of five adult daughters had an alcoholic mother. We are not sure of how many women alcoholics live in the United States, but we do know of many double-standard reasons for greater denial of alcoholism in women than in men. If you are an adult daughter of an alcoholic mother, you have probably had a hard time even finding information about yourself since most studies on adult children seldom compare the differences between sons and daughters of alcoholics, let alone daughters of alcoholic mothers as opposed to alcoholic fathers.

To understand the impact of gender differences on adult children of alcoholics, we need to consider not only the gender of the child, but also the gender of the alcoholic. The study of adult daughters on which this book is based did not find significant differences between daughters of alcoholic mothers and alcoholic fathers regarding the degree to which either group identified with characteristics of adult children (which are discussed in a later chapter). The overall scores between daughters with alcoholic fathers and mothers are about the same, but when you examine which characteristics and behaviors each group identified with, differences emerge. In other words, based on which parent was alcoholic, the groups differed on what bothered them more. Statistics did not tell the whole story, but listening to adult daughters' perceptions of the differences filled in many gaps.

Through interviews and clinical observations, strong differences are apparent between daughters of alcoholic mothers and alcoholic fathers on such things as their levels of emotions, what problems they identified for themselves, their attitudes about the alcoholic parent and their recovery issues.

Adult daughters of alcoholic mothers shared that their mothers' drinking strongly affected seven areas of their lives. Some of these areas related directly to their relationships with their mothers, while some areas related more to the daughters' own self-esteem or abilities to relate to other people. As you read these concerns of adult daughters, you may be inclined to think that the problems are common in many mother-daughter relationships, even among nonalcoholics. That observation is true, but the *degree* to which they exist and how they developed because of alcoholism make them unique and more difficult for adult daughters. As discussed in earlier chapters, alcoholism alters normal interaction patterns.

The seven issues that daughters of alcoholic mothers most commonly focus on are role models, relationships, parenting, identity, trust, trying to please and shame. We discuss each of these in the order of frequency in which adult daughters of alcoholic mothers mentioned them.

Role Models

That adult daughters of alcoholic mothers mention role-model difficulties as the most common problem is not surprising. Our gender identifications traditionally come from identifying with people of the same gender. Daughters of alcoholic mothers consistently state that their mothers' role performance made them angry, disappointed and confused.

Some of this anger may have been directed inward, creating additional problems for the adult daughter. For example, one of the behaviors that their mothers modeled was how to drink. Not surprisingly, the highest rates of concern about their own alcohol and drug usage came from adult daughters of alcoholic mothers.

The inability of their mothers to responsibly fulfill their parenting roles bothers many adult daughters, who often state that they did not feel that they had received proper nurturing or maternal support. In fact, many adult daughters feel that the roles between them and their mothers were reversed. Adult daughters often state that they did not receive anything from their mothers, but that the daughters themselves were the ones expected to provide constant care.

I wanted comfort and love from her, but she was either angry, resentful, irritable, or drunk and needing to be taken care of, put to bed, etc. I had and have lots of feelings of disgust for my mother as an alcoholic.

Mickey

The inability of mothers to fulfill their responsibilities led many daughters to share that they resented having so much responsibility of their own at such an early age. They often state that they were forced into taking over the female role in the house. "I had to become the mother" is a comment often made. Unfortunately, this situation put many of the adult daughters at high risk for incest, too.

I had to take over the female roles in the family—caring for younger siblings, cleaning, cooking and sometimes being Daddy's sexual partner.

Beverly

Many adult daughters of alcoholic mothers silently were asking, *What do you do without having been taught and emotionally supported?* These adult daughters answered, *Hopefully, the best you can.*

Relationships

Not having a healthy relationship with their mothers is the most common type of relationship problem that adult daughters of alcoholic mothers mention. These daughters shared their concerns about not knowing how to relate to their mothers, no longer wanting to relate to them or feeling totally dominated by them.

Mom was a closet drinker. I always knew something was wrong, yet I could not place my finger on it. I was always attempting to "reconcile" with her and could never quite make it. How can I use her as a role model when I know she has a problem? When is what she says valid and when is it not?

Jane

Other daughters state that, as a result of their interactions with their mothers, they now find interacting with and trusting other women very difficult.

I have difficulty being friends with other women because I do not trust or believe that a woman values you as a friend. I always feel that women are the "enemy." I idolize the female, but I never find anyone "perfect."

Joyce

A common theme among some adult daughters of alcoholic mothers is anger with their mothers for indirectly teaching them how to tolerate abusive male relationships. This theme may emerge from the fact that almost half of all alcoholic women who enter treatment have been the victims of abuse in their relationships. If you witnessed your mother in an abusive relationship, did you unknowingly develop any attitudes that put you at a high risk for tolerating abusive males? Some adult daughters think so, and they are angry with their mothers for teaching them to be tolerant of such abuse.

I want to forgive my mom for teaching me to accept emotionally and verbally abusive men into my life. Mom accepted inappropriate behavior from my dad, and I learned to do the same.

Cher

Parenting Skills

Did you learn any parenting skills from your mother? Adult daughters of alcoholic mothers state that either they did not learn any skills, or that the ones they learned were negative.

> I was thirty-six years old and my mother had been dead for three years before I could convince myself I might possibly be a good mother. . . . My mother used to tell me she hoped I never had kids because they were such horrible ingrates. . . . I feel as if she cursed me. She used to tell my brother and me if we ever did anything she didn't like she would have us put in reform school or a mental hospital. . . . My mother has been dead four years, but I still have a hangover.
>
> *Claudia*

Responses from adult daughters of alcoholic mothers about parenting range from not wanting children at all to wanting to be the perfect parent. Many adult daughters state that they wanted to be there for their children because their mothers were not there for them. However, such statements as "I don't want any children," "I don't know how to parent," "How can I nurture my children when I have not been nurtured?" "I do the same things my mother did and I hate it," and "How do I relate to my own daughter?" indicate the difficulties shared by adult daughters of alcoholic mothers about their own parenting skills. Their messages carry a painful question: How do you do it when you haven't seen it done?

Identity

Having an alcoholic mother raised many gender identity issues for adult daughters—not issues related to sexual preference, but rather feeling comfortable with the gender identity of being female. "How do you develop your sexual and feminine identity?" is the most frequently asked question. Most adult daughters express that they did not receive positive gender modeling from their mothers. Adult daughters do not feel that they were exposed to conditions that allowed them to develop an appreciation for their own femininity, which often resulted in a poor self-concept not only for the adult daughter, but also about being a female. Intimate discussions and questions about sexuality never occurred for many adult daughters.

Additionally, the adult daughters may have picked up their mothers' concerns and doubts about their own gender identities, which alcoholism may have compromised. Many women alcoholics suffer from self-doubt about feeling feminine or fulfilling their roles appropriately. This feeling may have been passed on to the daughters, who were left with the doubts of their mothers as well as their own about gender identities.

> I have become aware that in rejecting my mother's alcoholism, I rejected her and did not embrace all that it means to be a woman and feminine as well. . . . I felt emotionally abandoned. We never had any mother-daughter talks.
>
> *Kathleen*

Trust

As stated earlier, many adult daughters admit to having problems trusting other women. This feeling appears to relate to not being able to trust their mothers and equating their mothers with all women. Other adult daughters feel that their trust problems are more related to themselves. They do not feel comfortable trusting their own feelings and believing that they perceived situations and people accurately, as if others held the conditions that established or destroyed trust in their lives. The result is a no-win situation for adult daughters of alcoholic mothers, who learned that they did not trust themselves and they could not trust their mothers either.

> I would go to bed and trust that everything would be okay in the morning. In the morning I would wake up and hold my breath until I heard my mother's words. If they came out pleasant, I took a deep breath, gave a deep sigh of relief, and then I could get on with my day.
>
> *Lynda*

Trying to Please

Did you ever feel inadequate because you tried so hard to please someone and they were never satisfied? If so, you can identify with the adult daughters of alcoholic mothers who share this concern. Not only did many adult daughters find themselves forced into taking over many mothers' duties, but also the daughters were chastised for not doing the duties properly. Adult daughters shared that they often felt emotionally trapped because they admitted that they tried to please someone who caused them to feel anger.

Imagine being on a merry-go-round of whoever gives away the most is the best, except that you keep going in circles. We know that one of the most mentioned concerns for adult daughters is riding the "I have to please everyone" ride. Trying to please others and be appreciated is one thing, but trying to please someone who not only denies you support, but also tells you that you are not good enough, is extremely painful. "No matter what I do, it is never good enough" soon becomes "*I'm* not good enough."

Shame and Fear

Adult daughters often express that they felt more shame having an alcoholic mother than an alcoholic father—another example of the gender double standards in our society—but this realization does not reduce painful feelings for the adult daughter. Adult daughters indicate that they went to great lengths to cover up their mothers' drinking. The finding that adult daughters did not want to admit having an alcoholic mother until they were almost nineteen validates this concern.

What is the greatest fear of adult daughters of alcoholic mothers? Growing up and becoming just like their mothers. Becoming an alcoholic, repeating parenting patterns and developing poor relationships are the greatest fears for adult daughters. Many adult daughters express that they had become even more aware of how unhealthy their mothers' behaviors were only when the adult daughters started to do them themselves.

When the heat is really on, my mother switches into "fuzzy" as I call it—gives erroneous responses to direct questions, seems confused and intellectualizes at a preschool level. Horror of horrors, I do the same thing and I hate it.

Lisa

If you had an alcoholic mother, you probably experienced much pain and received little support. Besides the issues mentioned above, one noticeable fact about the family dynamic stood out: Few adult daughters of alcoholic mothers mention their fathers. None of the daughters indicated that they could count on their fathers to help or offset the impact of their mothers' alcoholism. We know that only 10 percent of men will stay with an alcoholic spouse. However, of those men who stay, they do not appear to be able to help their daughters with the pain of having an alcoholic mother.

If you had an alcoholic mother, your feelings of extreme isolation, issues of gender identity, doubts as a parent and self-doubt are justified. Unlike daughters of alcoholic fathers, you are more likely to be confronted with your own gender issues in your recovery and more likely to be angry with your alcoholic parent.

Your greatest challenge in recovery will be to become your own healthy role model. However, you do not have to recover alone anymore. Look for healthy women with whom you can spend time. Let their health surround you and support you. Allow their role modeling to show you healthy ways to relate to yourself and others. You *can* value your identity and, more importantly, yourself. As you begin to grow healthier, your anger toward your mother will weaken. Yes, your mother was an extremely influential and important woman in your life and she dominated your childhood. Childhood is over, but are her dominance and example over? Who is the most important woman in your life now? *You are!*

I overflow with hope to know that beyond the angry feminist, beyond the silent housewife, beyond the temple prostitute, beyond the fearful little girl, there is a woman emerging. She is vulnerable and strong, vocal and receptive, active and inner, a mother, a wife, a person. She knows how to cry, to love, to dance and to forgive.

Cindy

AFTERTHOUGHTS

Mother loved all mankind, but she did not know
how to let her children love her.

ANNA ROOSEVELT

Hatred is a normal human feeling,
and a feeling has never killed anyone.

ALICE MILLER

Words are more powerful than perhaps anyone suspects,
and once daily engraved in a child's mind,
they are not easily eradicated.

MAY SARTON

I have a right to my anger, and I don't want anybody
telling me I shouldn't be, that it's not nice to be, and that
something's wrong with me because I get angry.

MAXINE WATERS

Do not join encounter groups. If you enjoy being
made to feel inadequate, call your mother.

LIZ SMITH

Chapter 6

Alcoholic Fathers:
Daughter Dearest*

*All of the quotes in this chapter are from adult daughters of alcoholic fathers.

Dad was a happy person when he drank. He would play with me and I could have anything I wanted. I learned early how to "wrap him around my finger" because I was "Daddy's girl." Today he is sober, but I still have a hard time dealing with him, as he does not want to talk about what it was like when I was growing up. It's like he has resolved things, but I'm not given the same opportunity.

Debbie

When I do workshops around the country on adult children, I always address gender issues. If possible, I divide the audience into groups. Each group focuses on specific gender combinations, such as alcoholic mother-adult daughter, alcoholic father-adult daughter, alcoholic mother-adult son, etc. The largest group is always the alcoholic father-adult daughter. Most of the time this group is so large that it is divided into smaller groups. After watching this disproportionate interest among adult daughters of alcoholic fathers, I was beginning to wonder if alcoholic families specialized in having daughters.

But as we discovered, women are more willing to support the growth of the children of alcoholics movement and appear to be more willing than adult sons to support their own growth. On the other hand, we know that we have more alcoholic fathers than alcoholic mothers in this country. Additionally, we know that 90 percent of nonalcoholic spouses will remain with an alcoholic male, usually due to a lack of viable support alternatives. Therefore, the strong interest of adult daughters of alcoholic fathers is not surprising.

Whether or not they are more aware of their concerns than adult daughters of alcoholic mothers, adult daughters of alcoholic fathers are much more willing to talk about these concerns and to share their feelings more openly. Perhaps talking about your father is easier than talking about your mother. Maybe adult daughters of alcoholic fathers do not feel as isolated as adult daughters of alcoholic mothers, or perhaps having an alcoholic father is a more common experience.

If you are an adult daughter, chances are your father was an alcoholic. Did having an alcoholic father in your childhood leave you with specific feelings, issues and lessons? According to the many adult daughters of alcoholic fathers interviewed for this research, the answer is a resounding *yes*.

Can you identify with any of these lessons that adult daughters with alcoholic fathers shared?

- I still want to understand my father. I still want his acceptance and approval.
- I want to love him, but I hate what he does.
- I have a low opinion of marriage and relationships. I fear I cannot find a successful relationship.
- I am aware that I have issues with my nonalcoholic mother.
- I have difficulty relating to males positively.
- I learned to tolerate too much inappropriate behavior from males.
- Am I good enough to be loved?
- She who gives away the most is the best.
- I find "healthy" males boring, and the "wrong" ones available.
- I never received enough attention.
- I missed not having a "father-daughter" relationship.
- I have difficulty expressing anger to my father.

Besides the above lessons, some other differences about adult daughters of alcoholic fathers became apparent. (Again, although many of these issues might be found in many types of father-daughter relationships, the degree to which they occur and how they are dominated by alcoholism makes them unique for adult daughters of alcoholic fathers.)

The way that adult daughters talk about their alcoholic fathers is very different from how adult daughters talk about their alcoholic mothers—not that both groups identify different issues, but rather *how* they talk about them. As you recall, adult daughters of alcoholic mothers express much anger and resentment and appear more "attacking" when talking about their mothers. Adult daughters of alcoholic fathers, however, appear to be more "defensive" when talking about their fathers and express a need to understand the father's behavior.

Although many fathers engaged in highly dysfunctional behaviors and caused much pain for their daughters, the desire to establish a relationship with him still exists in most cases. With some adult daughters, however, this desire was not present. They are extremely angry with their fathers and want to separate from them as much as possible. However, when an appropriate father-daughter relationship did not occur, as was usually the case, many of the adult daughters held themselves partially responsible for the lack of a positive relationship. In essence, adult daughters do not generally hold their alcoholic fathers totally responsible for their behaviors, but alcoholic mothers are held accountable or attacked for everything. Reasons for treating an alcoholic mother differently may be because of the unfair practice of the blame-the-mother syndrome, another example of our punitive double standards. We might feel more comfortable accusing our own gender than the opposite one, or a greater tolerance among adult daughters for their fathers' behavior may simply exist.

Daughters' Need for Fathers' Approval

Many adult daughters express a need for their fathers' acceptance and approval. Therefore, they are less likely to focus negatively or consistently attack those whose approval they want. To seek the approval of someone they attack could reflect negatively on them.

For example, going around publicly condemning someone and then expressing the need for that person's approval would raise the question of what kind of person you are. Therefore, to feel comfortable about wanting someone's approval, you must minimize their negative behaviors. This situation is kind of an emotional trap, and could become overwhelming if you think about it. (Scarlett O'Hara had to be a COA. How else could she have invented, "I'll think about it tomorrow"?)

For example, as a young girl your alcoholic father provided you with many mixed messages, such as "I love you, go away and leave me alone," or "You are expected to love me, and I am expected to do what I want." Now that you are an adult, mixed messages can still dominate your relationship with him.

> My dad to me was mixed messages: I love you, provide for you, call you Dolly, and yet I cannot talk with you or have an exchange of conversation. I cannot accept anger or conflict, yet I come across as angry and in conflict with each person in the family, including you.
>
> *Renee*

As an adult you can now carry these mixed messages inside of you. You might be feeling that you want to acknowledge the pain of his alcoholism on your life, but if you do, you no longer believe him to be a person worthy of approving you. However, his "approval trap" was very strong and silently controlled you. You no longer want him to emotionally control you, but he only related to you in a controlling manner. Thus, whatever relationship you may have, this means if you want to stay close, stay quiet.

Why would you want approval from someone who harmed you? Because that person controlled you? Most alcoholic fathers were found to be very controlling—emotionally, physically or both. Wanting the approval of someone who negatively affects you is the epitome of being in a controlling relationship. Again, you were probably caught in a mixed message or a no-win relationship. How do you get close to him and not be controlled, especially if the only behaviors that he approved of were designed to please him? Separating emotionally from a powerful and controlling father is difficult.

However, his control may not be the only form of control that you are feeling. You may be silently controlling yourself because you are holding yourself partly responsible for the quality of the relationship with your father. Therefore, if your relationship is poor and you believe that you are responsible, whether you are or not, you are suffering from "justifiable emotional homicide." You are being controlled externally by him and internally by your self. When this result occurs, the mixed messages of childhood become internalized. They become part of us, and as adult children we have difficulty overcoming these messages. These erroneous messages are given to us. We internalize them and then give them to ourselves. Wouldn't it be nice if we could give them back, or tell the sender to keep them to himself, because we are too healthy to listen?

Another difference between adult daughters of alcoholic fathers and adult daughters of alcoholic mothers is that alcoholic fathers usually created "longing" in their daughters.

Longing is a plea to be accepted and loved. Longing is a hunger, an emotional need that is not met. Above all, though, longing is not love. Many adult daughters expressed a longing for a positive father-daughter relationship and were aware when this need was not met. Longing may explain why many daughters defend their fathers' behaviors. Emotional hunger can distort your perceptions. Therefore, many daughters do not want to see their fathers as they were, but rather how they should be. This idealized version of fathers remains strong with many adult daughters.

> In my case I wanted him to be my "knight in shining armor." He did not live up to this and up until now, no man has ever been able to live up to my ideal.
>
> *Jennifer*

Relationship with Nonalcoholic Mother

While growing up with an alcoholic father, what did you think about your mother? Discussing the relationship with the other parent is another major difference between adult daughters of alcoholic mothers and fathers. Daughters of alcoholic mothers seldom mention their fathers. However, many adult daughters of alcoholic fathers openly discuss their relationships with their mothers and the many characteristics of that relationship.

Relationships with their mothers range from an appreciation for how much their mothers helped offset the problems of an alcoholic father, to holding their mothers accountable for the family problems. A frequent comment is that many of the mothers' behaviors established negative role models for them. Adult daughters are very aware of how their mothers' reactions to an alcoholic spouse negatively influenced their opinions not only about their mothers, but also about spousal relationships, expectations in marriage and attitudes about how to relate to males. This awareness was especially apparent if their mothers were highly codependent and engaged in many dysfunctional behaviors. In fact, research indicates that when a nonalcoholic parent is highly codependent, the effects on the children are the same as if the children had two alcoholic parents (Obuchowska, 1974).

> Many of my resentments and worst memories are with my nonalcoholic mother, who was sicker than my dad. I have no real relationship with my dad and that makes me sad. I believe this has caused problems in my relationships with men.
>
> *Susan*

In the course of observing and interviewing adult daughters of alcoholic fathers, the following issues also arose: relationships, role confusion, intimacy, a sense of self, sexual abuse and perfectionism.

Relationships

Does the relationship that you had as a child with your father affect your relationships with males today? According to the adult daughters represented in this book, the answer is *yes*.

Relationship issues—the most frequently mentioned problem for adult daughters of alcoholic fathers—were divided into two categories. One is the relationship that you had with your father and the other is current adult male relationships. For many adult daughters, these two issues are not separate, but rather one primary issue that affects the other.

My father rejected me. I was forty-eight years old before he ever gave me a birthday gift or card, and then I wondered why he was doing it now. In my marriage to an alcoholic, I have found the same rage for my husband that I have for my father.

Mary Lou

What is or was your relationship with your father? Do you feel as if you had two relationships: one that was the actual relationship with your father and another that was your idea of how your relationship ought to be? If so, you are like most adult daughters.

One of the major problems of alcoholic fathers, according to their daughters, was that they never talked. They communicated very little and developed a feeling in their daughters that their fathers never really "knew" the daughter. Alcoholic fathers often lacked parental compassion and were emotionally unavailable.

For example, can you count on one hand the number of meaningful father-daughter conversations that you had? You may have wanted these talks to occur as often as possible, but he was not emotionally prepared or available.

This noncommunicating man manages to exercise a great amount of influence on his daughter. "Actions are stronger than words" is an understatement when describing many alcoholic father-adult daughter relationships. If you are like most adult daughters, however, you have probably hung in there with him and are hoping that you will someday have a more positive relationship.

What keeps you hoping? You eventually began to expect very little from him and thus any attention took on significant meaning. Many adult daughters state that they eventually believed that they "understood" their fathers better than anyone else. This empathy often included defending his behaviors to others.

Understanding him might have resulted from your abilities to read correctly and anticipate his moods and behaviors. This skill is developed in many children of alcoholics at an early age because your physical or emotional survival each day depends upon intuitions of how you should act and react. Unfortunately, these behaviors match those for the development of codependency.

Fathers often supported this understanding behavior in their daughters. Usually the father was not aware of her motivation, which was to deal with his ineffective parenting. Therefore, she would do what she could to establish some kind of a relationship. If you did this, you probably engaged in a lot of behavior designed specifically to please your father. If you could please him by your actions or words, he at least communicated something to you. He would interpret your behaviors not as pleasing him, but understanding him. Usually he used this approach in arguments with your mother by stating that, "At least my *daughter* understands me."

His motives for accepting your behavior were usually selfish and designed to maintain his denial of alcoholism. Your motives were probably to feel closer to him. If your father deprived you of attention and approval, you might have searched for ways to achieve it. Some daughters eventually gave up and others are still trying.

The legacy of an alcoholic father for most adult daughters can be found in their opinions about males or in their male relationships. In fact, in discussing relationships with adult daughters, relationship problems with other men are expressed more than problems with their fathers.

It's so strange, almost indescribable. My father is an alcoholic. My husband is not, but I still frequently find myself waiting for my husband (almost expecting him) to begin to display some of the

behaviors my father did. Sometimes it seems like I'm pushing him
to be like my father, whose behavior I hated.

Kelly

As you might suspect, most adult daughters express concern
about how to relate to males because of the influence of
their fathers.

What are your opinions about male relationships? What
are your opinions about males? Are you attracted to healthy
males or do you find them boring? Are you attracted to
unavailable males? Is a husband something you think you
should have, but you're not sure why? Your answers to these
questions may be based on how your father directly or indirectly fostered your ideas about men.

The greatest fear that adult daughters express is that they
will wind up in a relationship similar to their parents'. This
result was not surprising given that only 11 percent of adult
daughters rated their parents' relationship as above average.
Adult daughters, therefore, shared their issues with and concerns about males in the following ways:

- How to relate to controlling men
- Understanding healthy relationships
- Distrust of males
- Looking for Father in their relationships
- How to have a male friend
- No male is good enough
- Seeking unavailable men
- Addicted to relationships

Role Confusion

Adult daughters of alcoholic mothers refer to their exas-
peration over the poor role modeling they observed in their

mothers. Adult daughters of alcoholic fathers, however, share that their fathers were often poor role models, but talked about their own role confusion more. In other words, adult daughters state that they were unsure of their roles in the family. This feeling was largely the result of the vagueness of emotional and physical boundaries of interaction in the family between their fathers, their mothers and themselves. Did you ever feel caught in the middle in your parents' relationship?

Many adult daughters express role confusion because, with an alcoholic father, they often felt that they were taking the place of their mother.

For example, some adult daughters state that their mothers were emotionally absent and full of resentment toward their fathers. This situation caused the fathers to expect that their daughters understand them and support them. In many ways, the fathers responded to their daughters with "emotional incest."

Emotional incest occurs when a parent shares information with her or his child that should be shared with the spouse. Many adult daughters talk about becoming their fathers' emotional confidante. This type of interaction produced confusion for many daughters about where her role as daughter stopped and her role as adult emotional supporter started. For a child or a young woman, this role is inappropriate.

Mom rejected Dad sexually in their mid-forties, so Dad and I became emotionally incestuous. I need to learn to set emotional and sexual boundaries with men. I need to be assertive with my needs toward men and not fear losing them.

Marian

Intimacy

"I have a lack of self-esteem with men." "I fear failure in my relationships." "I am looking for a man to love me." "I lack closeness with men and I sacrifice myself to keep a relationship." Do any of these comments sound familiar to you? These statements reflect many of the concerns of adult daughters about their ability to achieve intimacy in their relationships. Many adult daughters hold their relationship with their fathers accountable for these problems.

> My search for intimacy? I spent a lot of years of my life, especially adolescent years, looking for a boy to love me, but not sexually. My father never talked with me. He never really talked to me at all, but he loved me. I know that he did. . . . I had to reach out to external sources for acceptance, guidance and strength.
>
> *Colleen*

Do you feel that your father really did love you, but he was not good at expressing it? If so, what did you learn about intimacy? Did you learn that intimacy was difficult to express? Did you learn that you could express it, but that it was okay if he didn't? Did you learn that your intimacy needs were not as important as his? Under these conditions, intimacy is a one-way street. You can leave your house and go somewhere, but you can't return. Your father may have loved you, but you may not have developed the most important ingredient required for intimacy, which is the ability to receive it.

> I am furious because my father made me his emotional spouse. I could never be me, never be sad or angry or have any negative feelings because he was so selfish and needy.
>
> *Marla*

Are you afraid of intimacy? Fear of intimacy is another problem that adult daughters share. They state that they had developed very low opinions or expectations about intimacy. Others indicate that they equate being intimate with not being in control and being too vulnerable. Fear of intimacy resulted from not being accepted by their fathers or having attempts at intimacy rejected.

> What I realized was that I had developed a fear of intimacy, and that subconsciously I was keeping my husband at a distance. I was afraid of becoming too close and giving myself to him completely because in the back of my mind I knew that I would be rejected. So if I didn't give myself completely, then I couldn't be completely hurt.
>
> *Estelle*

Sense of Self

> I think you have to accept yourself as a woman, and probably more importantly, a person. You have to realize that you are important as yourself and not an extension of another person.
>
> *Sherri*

For adult daughters to question their feelings about themselves is not uncommon. Alcoholic fathers often instill in their daughters problems of self-concept and self-esteem. Adult daughters of alcoholic fathers share that they secretly find valuing themselves—feeling good about themselves—difficult, which may explain the strong need for approval and acceptance from their fathers. When approval or acceptance is withheld, we are left to our own interpretations about ourselves. If we do not have an adequate internal sense of self-worth, we are not sure about our own performances. With this lack of security, we look outside ourselves for identity and worth. Constantly wanting your father's approval in order to feel good about yourself keeps you externally focused.

My father was a silent, shy, passive alcoholic, so I never knew how I stood with him. I usually thought his thoughts about me were negative. I was surprised when he told my husband I am his favorite child. I am the oldest of four.

Michelle

How do you feel about meeting your own needs? Are you comfortable meeting your needs, or do you feel more comfortable meeting the needs of others? Do you feel guilty if you think about yourself first? Many adult daughters of alcoholic fathers display an overly developed sense of guilt. These feelings are related to guilt about who you are, your self-worth and even your sexuality. Developing a strong sense of self comes from a well-integrated set of emotional parts.

For example, when you feel good about your ability to believe in yourself, your abilities to contribute to others, your abilities to take care of yourself and who you are as a person, you have a well-balanced sense of self. Many adult daughters state that their interactions with their fathers kept them off balance.

My father destroyed my healthy sexual image of myself. When I was a teenager, twelve or thirteen, and started to like boys, he said they were like dogs sniffing around if they showed any interest. I became ashamed of my sexual feelings and later felt pretty worthless. I got into a sexual affair with a boy at college because I didn't have any regard for myself. I did a lot of things in college I am ashamed of and realize now that it was because of total lack of self-esteem. I still haven't completely forgiven myself.

Dawn

Sexual Abuse

Unfortunately, almost 20 percent of adult daughters indicate that, while they were growing up, sexual abuse occurred in their families. These adult daughters were raised in double jeopardy and experienced twice the amount of victimization. All of the fear, rage, anger and emotional impact of being sexually abused dominated their childhoods. Although virtually all adult children feel that their childhoods were taken from them, sexually abused adult daughters also share loss of identity, personal boundaries, emotional support and personal security.

If you were sexually abused as a child, your recovery takes on so many other dimensions besides having an alcoholic parent. Sexually abused adult daughters feel that their fathers totally betrayed and emotionally abandoned them. Research findings indicate that the closer the sexual abuse victim is emotionally to the perpetrator, the greater the emotional damage. Most sexually abused adult daughters indicate that while growing up they didn't know where to turn for help. Additionally, because of all of the dysfunctional behaviors in their alcoholic families, adult daughters felt even more isolated.

Perfectionism

Are you a perfectionist? "Absolutely not. I just do things better than anyone else." Sound familiar? Always wanting to please makes you do the best that you can. However, you are probably never satisfied unless the outcome is "the best."

If you wanted your father's approval, how did you get it? By being the best? Or if you didn't have his approval, was that because what you did was not good enough?

I followed my father's career. I was a high achiever, went on to law school, worked in the office trying to do everything perfectly. . . . It was probably the best way for me to get his attention and his approval. That's why I adopted everything he thought and believed, because then I knew I was safe. If I agreed with him, then he was happy.

Marcy

Perfectionism develops from a desire to want to be perfect, but perfect in whose eyes: yours or someone else's? Usually the answer is "someone else's." Have you ever accomplished a task and someone else points out how wonderful or perfect the result is? What do you do? Do you agree or do you show them the flaws that you know exist? If you point out the flaws, you probably want to be perfect for someone else. For adult daughters of alcoholics, this person was often the father. You may have tried to live up to his ideal of the perfect daughter.

Overcoming perfectionism is not easy, especially if your natural inclination is, of course, to do it perfectly. Why does perfectionism have such a hold on so many adult children? Perhaps we have not learned enough ways to be valued or to feel good about ourselves. Therefore, if we are perfect in the eyes of someone else, we are at least acceptable to ourselves.

I always did the best I could do, but it was never good enough. If I made a B, I should have made an A. If I cleaned the house real good, my dad would move the furniture and say I didn't clean behind the furniture so it wasn't good enough. So in my own life everything is in place because then that means that I've got it all together and things are good. If things are out of place, something is wrong.

Althea

In spite of the many issues, in spite of the pain, in spite of his behavior, in spite of how he treats your mother, do you still want a father-daughter relationship? Would you still like to have his acceptance and approval? Would you like to know that he loves you for who you are and respects you? If you answer "yes," you are like the majority of adult daughters of alcoholic fathers.

Perhaps, however, the most important question is, if you cannot or will not be able to establish this relationship, will you go on and become as healthy as you can? Changing will not be easy. Even when we change, we want others' approval. Herein lies your hope. Although his approval was and still is important to you, if your father's approval is not available or comes in an unhealthy form, many other sources and many other people can provide you with a healthy sense of approval. Having approval from other places does not diminish your desire for a relationship with your father, nor does that approval make you a less-than-perfect daughter. Rather, you are a healthier human being to know that you have alternatives, that you have the potential for growth that someone else's inability to offer approval cannot limit. Of all the people in your life today, who is most likely to give you the healthiest and the most honest approval about yourself and your behaviors in order for you to grow? *You are!*

I am the most important one whose love and approval I need. Let go of looking for love and approval outside yourself and give it to yourself. . . . Through this I have found a deep underlying strength. I have an ability to take care of myself on an emotional level. The ways in which I have done this may not have been the most growth-promoting, but if I've learned those behaviors, I can learn others. . . . I have found a lot of positives waiting under the surface, and if going through this is how I came to these realizations, that's fine. As long as I know more of my own worth now.

Elizabeth

AFTERTHOUGHTS

My father was often angry when I was most like him.

LILLIAN HELLMAN

"Are you lost, Daddy?" I asked tenderly. "Shut up," he explained.

RING LARDNER

I wanted him to cherish and approve of me, not as he had
when I was a child, but as the woman I was,
who had her own mind and had made her own choices.

ADRIENNE RICH

It's clear that most American children
suffer too much mother and too little father.

GLORIA STEINEM

My father is home, working in the cellar. I sit on the steps and
watch. He asks why I don't go outside and play, but playing is dull
beside the excitement of being with him. Times I am allowed to
enter his world stand out like sentences highlighted in yellow.

DEBORAH TANNEN

Chapter 7

Two Alcoholic Parents: Don't Add, Multiply*

*All of the quotes in this chapter are from adult daughters of two alcoholic parents.

I'm an adult daughter of two alcoholics who attempts to take care of the world. I know that I must let go if I'm to live. I take life too seriously. I'm afraid of having my own kids. I don't know how to be a parent. My spouse drinks heavily. I find myself in a vicious circle. I'm continuing the patterns and I'm tired. Yet I don't know if I have the courage to change. I know the steps. Like a good ACOA, I've read all the books, but this time I don't know if I can fix it.

Winifred

Almost everything that was said in the last two chapters about having an alcoholic mother or an alcoholic father applies to adult daughters with two alcoholic parents. One thing that can be said about adult daughters of two alcoholic parents, however, is that their experiences were much more intense. According to adult daughters with two alcoholic parents, they consistently report that their problems were much more critical, they had greater feelings of despair, and felt even more unsure of how to recover than did adult daughters of one alcoholic parent.

If you are an adult daughter of two alcoholic parents, you certainly identify with many of the problems of all adult daughters. However, just as adult daughters of alcoholic fathers or mothers have their own unique problems and concerns, so do daughters of two alcoholic parents.

For example, as a daughter of two alcoholics you represent only one out of every five adult daughters. Therefore, you are likely to experience even stronger feelings of isolation and uniqueness. Daughters with only one alcoholic parent may have had a nonalcoholic parent who was able to help them. Probably you received no such help and therefore you had to rely on yourself even more. Did this make you feel even more isolated?

How do you teach yourself self-esteem? How do I encourage myself? Will I ever believe I'm okay? Thank God for the ACOA meetings and the literature on the market.

Vickie

According to Carol Williams and her work with alcoholic families, two alcoholic parents led to a much higher risk of physical child abuse. Thus, you may have been victimized physically as well as emotionally. Additionally, Williams found that the quality of childcare was lower in families with two alcoholic parents (1983).

Adult daughters of two alcoholic parents do not identify with the problems of both parents equally. Adult daughters commonly identify more strongly with the issues of the opposite-gender parent. While you likely felt concern for your mother or at the very least were affected by her, you probably focused more on the problems associated with your father's drinking. Some adult daughters, however, state that they find it very difficult to separate their problems between their mothers and their fathers.

My mother is now deceased, which gives me a different perspective on my problems. Strangely enough, my problems stem more from my relationship with my father. I'm an only child of older parents. Did he expect me to make it all better for him, too? He's a daily drinker. During later years we did talk about Mother's problem when she wasn't eating properly. I think I'm still trying to have a relationship with him—such a waste!

Florence

Rather than discuss the same issues that were found in adult daughters with one alcoholic parent, in this chapter we focus on those issues for adult daughters of two alcoholic parents, which were more intense and obviously more painful.

Research indicates that adult daughters of two alcoholic parents identify more strongly with the following six concerns than did adult daughters of one alcoholic parent:

- Relationships
- Children
- Relationships with parents
- Alcohol or drug use
- Spouse's alcohol or drug use
- Parents' sobriety

Relationships

Having two alcoholic parents produced lower levels of emotional satisfaction for adult daughters than having one alcoholic parent. If you had two alcoholic parents, how well have you handled your relationships? An indicator of relationship problems is that adult daughters with two alcoholic parents are less likely to marry, but much more likely to divorce. Many adult daughters stated that they were afraid of relationships because they never witnessed any parts of a healthy one.

As I answered these questions from an adult daughter perspective, I realized how difficult it was to separate the problems that resulted from the fact that my parents would have been dysfunctional even without the alcohol. They came to each other with their marriage already damaged and were unable to help each other grow. The alcohol added another dimension.

Myrtle

Children

Fear of parenting is very high for adult daughters of two alcoholic parents. Many of these daughters express fears that range from not having children at all to how to raise healthy children given limited parenting skills. Wanting to be a "perfect" parent is also a major concern.

> This adult daughter was so tired of parenting my parents that I vowed not to have children and did not.
>
> *Patricia*

Other concerns of adult daughters of two alcoholic parents about their parenting involve being too controlling, not knowing how to parent, lack of consistency and not being able to nurture their children. Although almost all adult daughters shared these concerns, they were especially evident for adult daughters of two alcoholic parents.

> My biggest fear is that I will hurt my children and that I will repeat or have been repeating the very same behaviors, which I felt hurt me, that my parents displayed. I am overly aware of my emotions and feelings, and I try hard to help my children express theirs.
>
> *Eileen*

Relationships with Parents

How well do you get along with your parents? How well do your parents get along with each other? Both of these questions are important concerns to daughters of two alcoholic parents. On the one hand, adult daughters say that in spite of all of the problems, they would still like to have a relationship if possible. Adult daughters of two alcoholic parents

are much more sensitive to the absence of a good relationship with their parents. Good times between you and your
parents or even one of your parents were too few, if at all.

Absence of criticism was the closest thing to praise I ever
received.

Chooch

Do you still find yourself hoping or doing things that you
think will help your parents to have a better relationship?
Marital problems in alcoholic families are a norm, but in
cases where both spouses are alcoholic, "problem" might be
an understatement. Daughters with two alcoholic parents
experience even more marital tension and problems. Many
adult daughters believe that their parents having a better
relationship would help tremendously. Does this sound familiar to you? Many young children of alcoholics follow this
same pattern. While you were young, did you do things hoping that you could help improve the relationship between
your parents? For many adult daughters of two alcoholic
parents, they are still trying and still hoping.

Alcohol or Drug Use

Higher rates of alcohol and drug problems are found
among adult daughters of two alcoholic parents than adult
daughters of only one alcoholic parent. Daughters with alcoholic mothers were also at a greater risk for alcoholism than
were daughters of alcoholic fathers (Niven, 1984). Having an
alcoholic mother not only placed the adult daughter at a
higher genetic risk, but having an alcoholic father also com-
bined to place her at a greater role-model risk. Additionally,
Sharon Wilsnack found that women's drinking patterns

strongly relate to the drinking patterns of their husbands, siblings and friends (1982). This finding confirms that adult daughters of two alcoholic parents present a higher risk for drug and alcohol use because so many adult daughters married a spouse who later developed alcoholism.

I am a recovering alcoholic of two years. I have been in individual therapy for three years, and I have just started a women's ACOA therapy group. Through my AA recovery, therapy and my last relationship, I am finally becoming aware of my patterns in relationships and that I need to focus on me now. It is very frightening to be alone, but I have hope. I have run in every way possible from myself, and now I am beginning to stop.

Lee

Spouse's Alcohol or Drug Use

A common belief is that adult daughters disproportionately marry alcoholics. This statement is partially true, but also biased. Although many adult daughters find themselves in an alcoholic marriage, they did not find themselves an alcoholic to marry! Few women ever marry an active alcoholic. Adult daughters disproportionately marry males who *become* alcoholic. Unknowingly, adult daughters, especially adult daughters of two alcoholic parents, may marry males who are at a very high risk for alcoholism. Given these high risks, no wonder you may be in a relationship with someone who is addicted or someone who is overly controlling. Perhaps you are in a relationship with a high-risk male, such as the son of an alcoholic. Regardless of the situation, we know that adult daughters of two alcoholic parents are highly concerned about the alcohol and drug use of their spouses.

It has been like wearing blinders. I put them on in order to survive, but they prevented me from seeing alcoholism developing in
my husband or being able to talk with my daughters about it.

Mimi

Parents' Sobriety

As is the case with all adult daughters, a desire for their
parents' sobriety is a strong concern. For adult daughters of
two alcoholic parents, this concern is even stronger. As great
as this desire is, adult children cannot recover for their parents, no matter how much they try. If you could get sober for
your parents, you would have done it years ago. Do you
accept the reality that you cannot recover for them, or are
you still taking on the responsibility for getting them sober?

Besides the above areas of concern, remember that adult
daughters of two alcoholic parents also share the problems
of intimacy, role confusion, sexuality, perfectionism, identity,
trust and trying to please others that are found among adult
daughters of alcoholic fathers or mothers only. If you are an
adult daughter of two alcoholic parents, your road has been
far more difficult, your issues more intense and the experience has more likely exhausted you.

As an adult daughter of weekend alcoholic parents, I feel very
emotionally burned out. I have a hard time dealing with personal
problems in my life. I feel very physically and emotionally tired,
which is not usual for someone who was always very active and
ready to attack problems head-on. I feel cheated in that my childhood was stolen from me and I had to take on adult responsibilities at such an early age.

Diane

Adult daughters of two alcoholic parents have shared that
recovery depends upon the ability to rely on inner strength.

At the same time, these adult daughters state the awareness of the need to be around healthy people to help draw them out and to provide healthy role models.

Be patient and compassionate and respect your own growth process. Make conscious decisions to be 100 percent responsible for your own life and focus on being in mutual relationships, which nurture and support. Allow yourself to feel your feelings, especially anger, and create a nurturing supportive network of people for yourself. Look for information, but trust your inner voice for your life's direction and purpose.

Toby

AFTERTHOUGHTS

*If you cannot trust your father and mother to love you
and to accept you and protect you, then you are an orphan,
although your parents are upstairs asleep in their beds.*

ELIZABETH FEUER

Pay attention to what they tell you to forget.

MURIEL RUKEYSER

*The kind of beauty I want most is the hard-to-get kind that
comes from within—strength, courage and dignity.*

RUBY DEE

*There are no hopeless situations; there are only people
who have grown hopeless about them.*

CLARE BOOTHE LUCE

*My father would come home and say, "You did well,
but could you do better? It's hard out there."
I would come home from school with a good grade
and my father would say,
"Must have been an easy assignment. . . ."*

HILLARY RODHAM CLINTON

Chapter 8

Secrets and More Secrets

If it had just been the drinking, I think I would have been okay.
Lillian

In alcoholic families some issues are even more secret than the alcoholism. Often the associated behaviors in alcoholic families contributed to not only more problems, but these problems also meant even more pain and confusion for adult daughters. Three of the most common extra problems for adult daughters are parental divorce, abuse in the family and eating disorders. In this chapter, we discuss these three problems and see that all three have many issues in common with each other and with alcoholism. However, one of the most important things that all these problems have in common is that adult daughters often tried to keep others from knowing about them. Adult daughters' lives became filled with secrets and more secrets.

Having and keeping secrets can be a magical part of childhood. Many of the women I interviewed told me that having secrets was a great part of growing up and being girls. These women, however, were referring to the positive side of secrets. For example, secrets often build close and trusting relationships between friends. They bound girls together. People who share a secret can have a sense of togetherness and a sense of power. Knowing who you can trust with a secret helps to develop skills of character judgment. To keep a secret you need to learn how to protect it and be faithful to a friend. Some women told me that their best friends today are still ones who shared secrets with them when they were young. Finally, a positive side of secrets is that they can be fun, even if the fun is just as simple as, "I've got a secret . . . na-na, na-na, na, na!"

The negative side of secrets, however, can cause significant pain. Unlike the positive side of secrets that can bind you with others, the negative side can separate you from others. Instead of developing closeness, secrets develop feelings of isolation. Alcoholism, divorce, abuse and eating disorders are all situations that involve the negative side of secrets. Unlike the secrets of childhood, which often involve sharing girl-to-girl, the secrets of these situations involve sharing secrets with and about adults, which is not bad in and of itself. With a negative secret, though, the child loses so much. For example, the benefit of having a loving adult in your life whom you can depend on is lost. Trust is destroyed. Your relationship with the adult is now based on fear of discovery. No matter what you do together, even if the activity is supposed to be enjoyable, the burden of the secret is always present, becoming the focus of your relationship.

> My life as a daughter of an alcoholic was one huge secret. What happened in my home on a regular basis, utter chaos, was never revealed to friends or teachers. I lived two lives.
>
> *Kathy*

Adult daughters of alcoholics who were sexually abused are even more aware of the pain and destruction of secrets in their lives. Catherine Cameron, in her book *Resolving Childhood Trauma*, writes about how women who were sexually abused often were made to feel like accomplices to the secrets (2000). These women felt that not only did the secret cast a shadow on them, but also that revealing the secret would be costly to themselves and to others. The sexually abused fear what others might think of them and the stigma of sexual abuse. Additionally, they fear that if they told anyone about the abuse, they would further destroy their families, have someone arrested or cause their parents to divorce. For example, consider the number of secrets in the following story shared by Laurie, an adult daughter of an alcoholic father.

The sexual abuse started when I was age twelve. It lasted for approximately one year. I thought I was doing something to cause what was happening. My father told me if I did not keep quiet, he would leave my mother. The confusing part was my father was really a nice man when he wasn't drinking. I would not sleep at night until I knew he was home and passed out. I was afraid to tell anyone. At age thirteen, I planned to kill my father. I thought about how I was going to do it when he was on top of me. He came home drunk one night and came into my room. He would always call me in a mean voice, "Laurie." I pulled the gun from under the covers and shot him. I hit him in the shoulder. I'm forty-four years old now. My father died three years ago just before Christmas. He always claimed that he shot himself. He never came into my room again. No matter how I rationalize or understand, I have to live with the fact that I shot my father. I was the oldest and the only girl.

Laurie

Laurie's story has many secrets, none of them good. Laurie was required to keep several secrets. She kept the secret that she was sexually abused for many years. She indicated that she was afraid to tell. She kept the secret from her mother. She kept the secret that the person who abused her was her father. She made a plan to kill her father and kept it a secret. Can you imagine how afraid and hopeless she must have felt that her only alternative was to kill her father? No one knew that she shot him except her father, which was a secret that bound her to her father in an unhealthy way. Obviously, Laurie's father had several secrets to keep as well.

This story also demonstrates how adult daughters are often made to feel like accomplices. Laurie tells us that she thought she was doing something to cause what was happening. By not telling anyone, she became an accomplice in protecting her mother from not having her father leave.

Laurie was forty-four years old at the time of the interview. She worked in a program that helped women who were victims of sexual abuse and incest. Even though Laurie knew what she knew about sexual abuse and incest from working with other women and being a victim herself, she had difficulty moving past her own feelings of being a contributor—not only to the abuse, but in blaming herself.

Finally, we see that Laurie tries to protect her father. In spite of all that he has done to her, she tells us that when he was not drinking he really was a nice man. This statement represents Laurie's ultimate denial of her father's behavior and her desire to keep a secret. "Really nice" men do not rape their daughters!

Unspoken Rules of Troubled Families

Keeping secrets in your family and from others requires you to maintain a set of family rules. These rules are similar to secrets because they are unspoken. No one ever voted on developing the rules or what they should be, but everyone in the family helps to maintain them. These rules form the core of dysfunctional and troubled families. As the family develops more and more problems, more rules are needed to protect family secrets. Divorce, abuse and eating disorders—which are discussed in more detail later in this chapter—are not exceptions to these rules.

Unspoken family rules are often "shame-based," which means that you believe that what is happening reflects on you and your self-worth. You likely also feel ashamed about what is happening in your family and you want to keep it from others. Having a secret and feeling shame often go together for many adult daughters. In order to try to avoid both of these feelings, family members often practice a set of rules to reduce the chance of confronting secrets and the shame behind them.

Members of dysfunctional families not only learn these rules, but family members also learn to internalize them, so that the family rules become everyone's *individual* rules. Breaking them is like breaking a secret. Even though the rules are unhealthy, family members commonly maintain them in order to emotionally protect themselves and others.

Some of the most common rules found in families with alcoholism, divorce, abuse and eating disorders are similar to the eight rules of shame-bound families (Fossum, 1989). These rules include:

1. **Be in control at all times.**

In order to keep a secret, you need to be in control of who knows it, making sure that you don't tell anyone. Earlier in this book we talked about control and how people in highly controlling situations try to maintain their balance by becoming controllers themselves. Many adult daughters felt a strong need to try to control access to information about what was happening in their families and to themselves by trying to keep their emotions under control at all times. They believed that if they expressed their emotions about the trauma in their lives that they would "lose it" or let someone know the family secret.

2. **Always be right; do the right thing.**

On the surface, "doing the right thing" sounds like a good idea in a dysfunctional family. However, doing the right thing does not always mean doing the healthy thing. "Doing the right thing" in this context usually means pleasing the person who has the power and who is controlling the situation. In other words, many adult daughters were forced to go along to get along. Under these conditions, keeping the family secrets was perceived as doing the right thing. You may have survived using this tactic, but it didn't fool you. Anyone who is being abused knows that what is happening is not right.

3. **If something doesn't happen as planned, blame someone, yourself or another person.**

Placing blame is not a substitute for finding a solution. Blaming only postpones it. In order not to deal with the dysfunction in a family, the people in power divert the truth by finding someone to blame. Unfortunately, many adult daughters began to blame themselves for what was happening in their families. Placing blame, even on themselves, kept adult daughters from seeking help, but at least they believed that they were keeping the family rules. Yet they also were keeping secrets and hiding a lot of pain.

4. **Deny feelings, especially the negative or vulnerable ones, like anxiety, fear, loneliness, grief, rejection or need.**

A typical statement of adult daughters is, "I felt so vulnerable, like there was nothing I could do." Negative feelings can make you feel vulnerable, and denying them is a way to avoid that vulnerability. These adult daughters are the ones who earlier in the book stated that, "Nothing is wrong, but I don't feel right." Verbally they try denying their emotions, but they are left with a feeling that something is not right.

5. **Don't expect reliability or constancy in relationships.**

Life in addicted families is unpredictable. Parents typically won't be consistent in their behaviors. Family members often react to the alcoholic depending upon whether she or he is in a toxic or nontoxic condition. Abusive families just make things even more volatile. Strained parental relationships lead to inconsistent parenting.

Besides not being able to count on family members behaviorally, adult daughters often talk about the mood swings that occurred with their family members. One of the most typical examples of mood swings was how a crisis could be treated with intense feelings and then almost immediately people changed as if nothing happened.

Many adult daughters learned at a very early age not to count on anyone. Others learned that they never expected anything good to last very long. They were always waiting for the other shoe to drop. "Don't expect anything good to last very long in this house" became the family norm.

6. **Don't bring transactions or disagreements to completion or resolution.**

In the troubled family, nothing is ever resolved. Pain goes on without apologies, arguments are ignored, resentments build and people drift farther apart. More secrets occur when families never resolve anything because another huge secret becomes, "I'm mad at you, frustrated by you and feel abandoned by you, but I can't tell you. Besides, what good would it do? We never deal with anything."

This rule is also a form of denial that keeps people from reaching conclusions. No one wants to admit the obvious. The motivation behind this rule is that no one wants to deal with conflict. Additionally, each unresolved issue is added to another and another, and family members are afraid that confronting one issue will open a "can of worms."

7. **Don't talk openly and directly about shameful, abusive or compulsive behavior in our family.**

This rule is the basic "elephant in the living room." No one wants to admit that an elephant is in the living room, but everyone feeds it and walks around it. No one wants to openly address the drinking, abuse, fighting, tension and other problems that the family experiences. "We don't talk about those things," or "What are you talking about? There's no problem" are common statements.

The effect of this rule is that people endure pain in silence. As a child in such a family, an adult daughter learned early on that no room existed to talk about what was happening in her house; the place was too crowded with denial. Certain subjects—anything shameful or embarrassing—were considered off-limits.

8. **When disrespectful, shameful, abusive or compulsive behavior occurs, disqualify it, deny it or disguise it.**

The effect of this is to take the obvious and pretend that it is something else. "Dad didn't flip out on Mom and hit her; he's just under a lot of stress," or "Mother's not alcoholic; you know she only has a drink to relax a little before dinner" are both disqualifying statements. The idea is that if you disguise something you might not have to deal with it. One of the most common disqualifying statements about an alcoholic family member is when someone says, "She/he is not that bad yet," when trying to deny that someone is obviously an alcoholic. Additionally, no one wants to define or explain "yet." This form of denial always changes to meet the situation.

Adult daughters of alcoholics know well all of the above rules of shame-based households. Those adult daughters who have also experienced parental divorce, family abuse and eating disorders know them even better. Many of these rules are passed from generation to generation of dysfunctional families. In many cases, adult daughters did not feel as if these concepts were just rules in their families, but that they took the effect of laws. These rules often made the lives of adult daughters painful and miserable, but at the same time the rules enabled protection and survival. These rules are legacies, and for some adult daughters they have dominated their entire lives from childhood to adulthood. Adult daughters who were abused as children were denied help because of these rules, and some adult daughters watched as these rules tore their parents apart. Adult daughters who have developed eating disorders now maintain and apply these rules to themselves as adults.

Abused Daughters

All alcoholic families are abusive because alcoholism is in and of itself an abuse of other people. In addition to the abuse inherent in alcoholism, however, many adult daughters experienced other forms of child abuse, such as physical abuse, sexual abuse, neglect and emotional abuse. Those daughters who witnessed spousal abuse were also abused, because to hurt someone a child loves is to hurt the child. Finally, sibling abuse cannot be ignored as a form of abuse. Remember the letter from chapter 1?

> Why didn't I feel safe with my mother? I felt hated by my mother and two brothers. . . . My mother raged with jealousy as she watched us leave every day; she never received any positive attention from my father. . . . My brothers felt that their father abandoned them; I was not a popular sibling with them. . . . My mother saw the bruises and the scratches on my body, but she seemed to think I deserved them. When my brother broke my hand during a ritual beating, she yelled at me and delayed taking me to the hospital for hours.
>
> *Shelley*

A comparison of adult daughters of alcoholics to women who were raised in nonalcoholic families shows that adult daughters were three times more likely to have been victims of physical abuse, four times more likely to have been sexually abused, twice as likely to have experienced emotional abuse, four times more likely to have been neglected and six times more likely to have witnessed spouse abuse (see Appendix). Although many forms of abuse can occur in an alcoholic family, the discussion here focuses on the various forms of child abuse that affected many adult daughters.

Does alcoholism *cause* child abuse? Statistics vary greatly depending on the source. However, alcoholism and child abuse occur together disproportionately. Additionally, the alcoholic is not necessarily the family member who commits the abuse. Sometimes the nonalcoholic spouse abuses a child out of frustration and tension. Either way, a lot of adult daughters were raised in and face overcoming the double jeopardy of alcoholism and child abuse. According to the Children of Alcoholics Foundation (1995), children who are at double jeopardy of both alcoholism and abuse were more likely to have intensified problems such as:

- Emotional and psychiatric problems—anxiety, depression, eating disorders, and feelings of insecurity and dependence
- Physical problems—obvious physical injuries as well as assorted health problems resulting from neglect
- Behavioral problems—running away, teen pregnancy, school problems and aggression

For many daughters victimized by abuse, although the abuse might have ended in childhood, the emotional trauma continues into adulthood. Abused adult daughters shared that they felt as if they were still at risk for many unwanted emotions and behaviors because of the abuse, especially and more intensely for adult daughters who had been sexually abused. Sexually abused adult daughters often state that they find themselves struggling with many accompanying problems.

Adult daughters who suffered neglect indicate having current problems with trusting other people and themselves, anger, impaired social skills, low self-esteem, alcohol and drug abuse, and physical problems. Physical abuse victims shared many of the same problems, plus feelings of powerlessness and coping skill problems. Sexual abuse victims, however, had many extra burdens, even beyond those of neglect and physical abuse. These adult daughters had issues with feeling betrayed and stigmatized, and they were often victimized again. Research shows that later assault of a female incest or sexual abuse victim is not unusual.

> When I was a child, I was the victim of child abuse. I was abused physically and verbally by my mother and sexually abused by my father. My counselor is working with me right now on the sexual abuse because most of it I've blocked from my mind. It hurts to remember some things, but it's a relief to have the blame taken off my shoulders.
>
> *Mimi*

Most difficult for sexually victimized adult daughters is developing a healthy sex life as an adult. Understanding the difference between sex and affection comes hard for sexual abuse victims. What actually is intimacy? How do you find it when you are afraid to trust? How do you overcome a fear of intimacy when you have been introduced to sex too early, let alone against your will? The pain and anger for sexually victimized adult daughters relates to the feelings that someone used them. The feeling of being treated like an object makes a victim feel used. Innocence has been stolen and the victim wants to cry out in rage, but tears drown the voice. Only silent screams emerge.

> I was convinced sex was love. When I was not having sex, I was not feeling loved.
>
> *Kayla*

Finally, abused adult daughters share concerns over two other issues, regardless of the type of abuse experienced.

1. **Fear of repeating the patterns as parents**
Many adult daughters are aware that abuse runs in families, passed from one generation to the next. Their fears of repeating their parents' patterns are often based on the poor parenting models discussed earlier. Adult daughters often indicate that they want to be healthy mothers but feel as if they are not well prepared. Additionally, many adult daughters are aware of their needs to work through their own issues before they could feel good enough about themselves to be good enough parents.

> No one protected me—emotionally, mentally or physically—from violence and sexual abuse. Because of it, I know I have it within me to kill anyone that would ever abuse my child, including me. For that reason, I decided never to have a child.
>
> *Tilly*

2. **Fear of marrying a violent or addicted partner**
Many abused adult daughters do not want to wind up in a relationship with an abusive partner. They often state that their abusive childhoods made relationships very difficult for them.

It's ironic. When I was growing up and my parents fought and my mom got beat up, I thought, *I will never let this happen to me.* But I was a child and had no place to go. As a married woman, here I am in the same situation. I didn't want this to happen to me, but I felt I had nowhere to go—that I was stuck, just as I was when I was a child.

Lee Ann

Child abuse was personal for the adult daughter. Parental alcoholism belongs to the parent and is something that the parent does. When you are abused, though, that event personally happens to you, which makes the trauma so much more difficult to handle. You can move away from an alcoholic, but you can't move away from yourself. Repressed memories for many adult daughters are not just limited to facing that a parent was alcoholic or abusive, but also that the effect was very personal indeed.

I have always felt damaged, like something was missing from me, like I was a sexual deviant and that no "normal" guy would want me if they knew these things. I felt I would never get what I wanted: to be loved by a man properly, for me, the little girl with the stolen innocence.

Glenda

Divorce

I was and still am a victim of drug and alcohol abuse. It all started in my childhood. Both my parents drank, and when they got drunk, they would have a big fight. They would throw things at each other and hit each other.

Claire

Alcoholism is disproportionately involved when couples divorce. Many adult daughters know this fact only too well, growing up most aware of the problems in their parents' relationships. For example, when adult daughters of alcoholics were asked for their perceptions about the quality of their parents' relationships, only 11 percent of them rated the relationships as above average. Adult daughters of nonalcoholic parents rated 41 percent of their parents' relationships as above average. Clearly, the problems for parents who divorce not only affect their relationships, but they are also obvious to the children. As a matter of fact, daughters in divorcing homes are more aware of the difficulties prior to separation than are sons. Additionally, the problems that this knowledge causes for the daughters usually do not change after the divorce. Sons of divorce were more likely to have conduct disorder problems, while girls were more likely to become depressed or have "overcontrolled" behavior. These problems are precursors for perfectionism and struggling for control in adult daughters' lives and the lives of the people around them.

> My parents finally divorced, I was nine and heard no explanation other than, "He didn't want you."
>
> *Brenda*

As young girls, adult daughters of divorce were faced with the same problems as all daughters of divorce plus the added burden of alcoholism. The most common problems for these daughters in childhood included difficulties such as parental loss, economic loss, more life stress, poor parental adjustment, lack of parental competence and exposure to interparental conflict. As a result of these divorce difficulties, daughters were faced with the following adjustment tasks (Wallerstein, 1983):

- Acknowledging the marital disruption
- Regaining a sense of direction and freedom to pursue customary activities
- Dealing with loss and feelings of rejection
- Forgiving parents
- Accepting permanence of the divorce and relinquishing longings for the restoration of the predivorce family
- Resolving issues of relationships

If you are an adult daughter who experienced divorce, how have these problems affected you today as an adult? Are you doubtful about marriage? Do you hold back in relationships because you are afraid to totally commit to someone? Has the cycle of divorce repeated itself and you too are now divorced? All these are legacies of divorce for many adult children, but for daughters of alcoholics, have you ever wondered about additional issues? Have you ever thought that had the drinking stopped, your parents would not have divorced? Did you ever wonder if had *you* been better, maybe your parents would not have divorced? Did you ever wonder why this had to happen in your family? These difficult and nagging questions are made worse for adult daughters because they have no answers. Their legacies are carried into adulthood, and many adult daughters can't get a divorce from the divorce.

Eating Disorders

Of all the secrets we have discussed about alcoholism, abuse and divorce, eating disorders were the most secret for adult daughters, perhaps because this secret was the most personal. The other problems in their families involved other people. The alcoholism and the divorce happened to other people, and the adult daughters were forced to endure the dysfunction. Even though abused adult daughters had something that personally happened to them, other people were involved. Keeping the secrets about abuse, divorce and alcoholism involved keeping secrets about other people. Eating disorders, however, meant keeping secrets about themselves.

> I had many secrets that I had to hide, and it became impossible for me to have any friends, at least close ones. I withdrew into myself and never spoke unless it was necessary.
>
> *Elizabeth*

Determining the cause of eating disorders in women is difficult. Most of the literature and research indicate that eating disorders might be a combination of biological or genetic factors, environmental or sociocultural factors, and psychological factors. However, one of the most common themes found in all of the causal explanations is the influence of family.

Eighty-five percent of eating disorders for women start while they are adolescents, and a high probability exists that they are still living at home when the problem starts. Eating disorders seem to occur more often in daughters of mothers with eating disorders. Also, sexual abuse is not uncommon in the backgrounds of women with eating disorders. Other factors include coming from a dysfunctional family and having personal relationship problems. Psychological characteristics such as perfectionism and an overemphasis on independence, control and autonomy often accompany the development of eating disorders. Other psychological characteristics include depression, anxiety, anger, loneliness, feelings of inadequacy and low self-esteem. These characteristics and factors are not only found in women with eating disorders, but are common among adult daughters of alcoholics, abuse and divorce.

Any correlation of adult daughters of alcoholics and eating disorders is not surprising. Although no theory totally explains the cause of eating disorders, for some adult daughters one aspect of their lives obviously led to the other. Eating disorders perhaps developed as an outcome of life experiences as an adult daughter. Many women are adult daughters of alcoholics. Within that larger group are women who are adult daughters of alcoholics and child abuse; adult daughters of alcoholics, child abuse and divorce; and adult daughters who experience any combination of these and who develop eating disorders as well. Adult daughters with eating disorders have been affected in many ways, but the most critical is that their eating disorders accompany them wherever they go. All adult daughters harbor great emotional pain, but the daughter with eating disorders must not only confront what other people did to her, but also what she is doing to herself.

Many adult daughters with eating disorders added to the secrecy of their lives. Bulimics often engage in their behavior in secrecy and then feel guilty about hiding their behaviors. Women suffering from anorexia nervosa seem to be in a constant pursuit of thinness that only they can define.

For women with eating disorders, yet another secret emerges that can often be referred to as "father hunger." As mentioned earlier in the chapter on alcoholic fathers, adult daughters frequently indicate that they wanted their fathers' acceptance and approval. Many alcoholic fathers were not able to meet this need, but that did not diminish the daughters in their longing for a relationship with their fathers. In her book *Father Hunger*, Margo Maine writes about the importance of a father in a girl's development (1991). Maine talks about the importance of emotional connectedness and unrequited love. Daughters who never felt that they were good enough for their fathers, or whose fathers were not capable of connecting with them in an approving way, experience much pain. Adult daughters with eating disorders are more likely to have alcoholic fathers than alcoholic mothers. Additionally, adult daughters who have eating disorders and alcoholic fathers are more likely to describe their fathers as emotionally distant than adult daughters without eating disorders.

Common Themes of Trauma

Child abuse, parental divorce and eating disorders all have one thing in common with each other and with parental alcoholism: trauma for its victims. Trauma survivors are often left with many feelings and issues. In her work with women and trauma, psychologist Tian Dayton describes some of the most common characteristics of women who are survivors of trauma (2000). Parental alcoholism, divorce, child abuse and eating disorders have obviously traumatized many adult daughters, and many are now dealing with the following characteristics:

Characteristic	Indicator
Learned helplessness	Losing the feeling that you can affect or change what is going on
Depression	Unexpressed emotion, agitated, anxious, feeling flat
Emotionally constricted	Numbness and shutdown as a defense against overwhelming pain and threat and a lack of range of expression of emotion

Characteristic	Indicator
Distorted reasoning	Convoluted attempts to make reason out of senseless pain
Loss of trust and faith	Deep ruptures in primary, dependency relationships and breakdown of an orderly world
Hypervigilance	Anxiety, waiting for the other shoe to drop—constantly scanning environment and relationships for signs of potential danger or repeated rupture
Traumatic bonding	Unhealthy bonding style resulting from power imbalance in relationships and lack of other sources of support
Loss of ability to take in support	Fear of trusting and depending upon relationships and emotional shutdown
Loss of ability to modulate emotion	Going from 0 to 10 and 10 to 0 without intermediate steps, rashness, loss of control, black-and-white thinking
Easily triggered	Stimuli reminiscent of trauma—e.g., yelling, loud noises, criticism or gunfire—trigger person into shutting down, acting out or intense emotional states

Characteristic	Indicator
High-risk behavior	Speeding, sexual acting out, fighting, relationship risks
Disorganized inner world	Disorganized object constancy and relatedness, fused feelings such as anger and sex
Survival guilt	From witnessing abuse and trauma and surviving, from "getting out" of a particular family system
Development of rigid psychological defenses	Dissociation, denial, splitting, withdrawal, aggression
Cycles of reenactment	Unconscious repetition of pain-filled dynamics
Desire to self-medicate	Attempts to quiet and control turbulent, troubled inner world through the use of drugs and alcohol

AFTERTHOUGHTS

Overcoming the far-reaching effects of child abuse is a painful, lifelong endeavor. But it has to begin with the first step: the truth.

LATOYA JACKSON

Most compulsive eaters hide their feelings as well as their food.

GENEEN ROTH

There is nothing Madison Avenue can give us that will make us more beautiful women. We are beautiful because God created us that way.

MARIANNE WILLIAMSON

In extreme youth, in our most humiliating sorrow, we think we are alone. When we are older we find that others have suffered, too.

SUZANNE MOARNY

The nature of this flower is to bloom.

ALICE WALKER

Part Three

Codependently Yours

Chapter 9

Me, Myself and I: How Well Do You Know These People?

Are you really different from other women? If so, what makes you different? Is it your personality, behaviors or characteristics, or do you "feel" different from other women without knowing why? On the other hand, if you do not believe that you are different from other women, and you are an adult daughter, how have you overcome many of the feelings and characteristics commonly associated with adult children?

The above questions have one thing in common: They both ask how well you know yourself. Are you aware of how your childhood experiences have influenced your behaviors and personality characteristics? Do you like what you know about yourself, or have you become the person that you never thought you would be?

This chapter discusses and uncovers your personality characteristics and the extent to which they are similar to or different from those of women from nonalcoholic families and from other adult daughters. Why bother to know your characteristics or behaviors? If you would like to change or recover from your childhood, you should know how and where you have been affected. Changing yourself is easier when you know where to begin.

On the other hand, have you ever considered that many of what you consider your negative behaviors can become strengths? Maybe you never thought of yourself as a person who has a lot to offer, or a person with competencies and personal assets. Maybe you never thought of yourself at all because you were too busy surviving or thinking and reacting to others. Well, enough thinking and taking care of others for now. Let's talk about you.

After recently reading a book about adult children, I identified so unbelievably and completely with characteristics of adult children of alcoholics. . . . I realized for the first time and understood where and how it had affected me. Oh, I cried, but to see how it had affected me and where my characteristics fit in was overwhelming. I think the tears that I felt were partly of relief . . . I had some reason for feeling lonely.

Madeline

Characteristics of Adult Children of Alcoholics: Do They Describe You?

Since the early 1980s, clinicians have observed certain personality characteristics that they attribute to adult children of alcoholics (Perrin, 1984; Woititz, 1983; Ackerman, 1991). The number of these characteristics typically has been around twenty. However, are these same characteristics found in other adults? For example, taking yourself very seriously is supposedly an adult child characteristic. Aren't there other adults who take themselves seriously? Isn't a certain amount of seriousness part of being an adult?

As we've seen throughout this book, if adult children really are different from other adults, the differences do not necessarily have to do with particular characteristics, but rather the degree to which these characteristics are found in adult children. Therefore, a more correct analysis is to say that these personality characteristics can be found in all adults, but are overly developed in adult children. Overdevelopment of these particular characteristics adds to the risk for developing certain problems.

To what extent do you identify with any adult children characteristics? Let's look at the twenty most commonly described characteristics about adult children and apply them to you. We'll look specifically at seven different "feelings" that the twenty characteristics measured. In other words, if you possess certain characteristics, how does that make you feel?

Additionally, many characteristics of adult children are related to each other. For example, the characteristics of taking yourself very seriously and experiencing difficulty having fun are associated with each other. If you identify strongly with certain characteristics, you probably have strong feelings about your needs as an adult child.

How obvious to you are your characteristics and how aware are you of the feelings that accompany them? Ask yourself the following questions in each section using this scale, 5 = always, 4 = often, 3 = sometimes, 2 = seldom, 1 = never.

Feeling Isolated

_____ I guess at what is normal.
_____ I feel different from other people.
_____ I have difficulty with intimate relationships.

Two of the most common feelings that adult daughters express are that they feel unique and emotionally isolated from others. These two feelings support each other. When you feel unique and different from other people, you become more isolated. Without adequate role models, you were on your own as a child to judge how "normal" people behaved in their relationships, friendships, parenting and intimate exchanges.

I didn't ever see myself as a game player. I tried to watch what other people did in order to maintain relationships. My role models were a mother who was wrapped up in her drinking and a father who was too wrapped up in my mother. I didn't really know what a normal relationship was. I would watch other people and mimic them. Literally, I would see what worked for the people on TV or in a movie, or my healthy friends, and I would actually mimic them. And I could never figure out why it didn't work for me.

Teresa

Inconsistency

_____ I have difficulty following projects through to the end.

_____ I look for immediate as opposed to deferred gratification.

_____ I manage my time poorly and do not set my priorities in a way that works well for me.

Do you sometimes feel as disorganized as your childhood? How can we be so controlling and yet feel inconsistent? If you spent a lot of your time meeting other people's needs, not much time was left for you. Finishing up your own projects and working on your own priorities were either done last or in a hurry when you had a "spare" moment. Rarely were they done in a logical or comfortable atmosphere.

Another reason for your inconsistency may be related to the usual amount of chaos that accompanies life in an alcoholic family. Judy Seixas refers to the alcoholic family as the "disorderly-orderly family" (1985). Everyone is trying to put consistency into an inconsistent environment, which is not possible in most alcoholic families. No crises are orderly and consistent, are they?

Self-Condemnation

_____ I judge myself without mercy.

_____ I have difficulty having fun.

_____ I take myself too seriously.

Are you tougher on yourself than other people are? Do you have two sets of standards? One set, which is accepting and kind, is applied to other people. The other set, which is excessively demanding and unforgiving, applies to you.

If you are overly self-critical and take yourself too seriously, you are at risk for self-condemnation. We can be so overly judgmental about our own behaviors that we can never please ourselves. Even when we do well, we don't believe it because of our negative self-outlook. The core of self-condemnation is having low self-esteem. Self-condemnation results from never feeling that you are good enough and that whatever goes wrong is your fault. When circumstances don't work out, you condemn yourself. This characteristic was found more commonly among adult daughters of alcoholic fathers rather than of alcoholic mothers (Berkowitz, 1988).

> I'm just now learning to have fun. That has meant taking some risks, too. It's difficult to sit down and write a list of even ten things that I would do that I consider fun things. A lot of things that I tend to see as fun things I would do alone.
>
> *Marge*

Control Needs

_____ I overreact to changes over which I have no control.
_____ I am either superresponsible or irresponsible.

Do you have a strong need to be in control at all times? Have you ever thought of what it is that you want to control? One's own desire for control was obvious to most adult daughters. However, what they want to control is not so obvious. That is, you have this feeling of needing to be in control at all times, but you are not sure of what you are trying to control.

Control issues for adult daughters were most likely to surface in one of three areas. Many adult daughters want to control situations and their surroundings. This form of control is closely related to your childhood, especially if you were the type of daughter who was trying to reduce the chaos in your family by taking charge of everything. Thus, if you were in charge, you were in control. If you were in control, you could make order out of chaos. Do you still feel a need to be in control of situations?

The second form of control occurs when you want to control relationships, either by your willingness to do more than your share in a relationship or by wanting guarantees from people that they will "never leave you." For example, if you do 75 percent of everything that needs to be done to maintain a relationship, you may believe that you are in control. With this division of labor, though, aren't you the one who is being controlled? Unfortunately, many times we believe that we as adult children are very controlling when in fact control is an illusion. If we were in control, why would many of these dysfunctional events be happening in our lives?

> I would try to control the outcomes and in turn I became very much codependent because I tried to control the other person—not only the outcome of the situation, but also the person. It was very draining, but I didn't have to look at myself.
>
> *Hannah*

The third type of control occurs when you want to maintain total control over your emotions. This control may have worked as a child in the alcoholic family for a while, but such attempts don't help your well-being as an adult. What do you do with your emotions? If you totally control them, does that mean that you do not express them? Probably so. Therefore, do you control your emotions, or in reality do they control you?

Wanting to control your emotions can be based on the fear that if you allow yourself to express them, so much may come forth that you will be out of control. Besides, you may have heard all of your life that you shouldn't "be so emotional" when in fact you have been holding in your emotions. "Don't be so emotional" means that you should deny your emotions.

Acknowledging my feelings is kind of scary for me. I get fearful that if I feel sadness that I'm going to withdraw into depression. . . . I fear that I'm going to fall apart. It's getting much better. I am able to cry more often now, and I let myself do that. I'm not falling apart, and it is acceptable and all right to feel sad. There is a big difference between feeling sad and feeling sorry for myself.

Agnes

Ask yourself, *What is the worst thing that could happen if I release my emotions?* Your answer likely represents your worst fear.

Releasing your emotions would likely be a positive experience for you. You will not only be releasing your emotions, but you will find parts of yourself that have been denied. They are *your* emotions: Express them, do what you want with them. Exchange your control and fear for release and growth.

Approval Needs

_____ I constantly seek approval and affirmation.

_____ I am extremely loyal even in the face of evidence that the loyalty is undeserved.

_____ I lie when it would be just as easy to tell the truth.

When we constantly want approval from others, we may be loyal to them even when they don't deserve loyalty. We often tell them what we think they want to hear, even if we have to lie. We are basically saying that any relationship is better than no relationship. If you want others' approval, what does their approval mean to you? Have you ever asked yourself why their approval is so important to you?

Many adult daughters feel that having the approval of others relates to their own self-esteem. With approval they could feel that they were doing the right thing and that they were accepted. A lower level of self-esteem may cause you to rely on others to provide external validation of your worth as a person.

> That was very frightening because I never knew what feelings I had because I avoided them. I had buried them and pushed them aside to please other people and to get other people's approval. As a result, I had to go through a lot of pain, and I'm still experiencing it.
>
> *Margaret*

A dilemma for most adult daughters, however, is that many of the people whose approval they want are not the healthiest people in their lives. For example, adult daughters share that they often want the approval of the alcoholic parent, or the person with whom they are in a relationship, even though they know that the alcoholic or their relationship person causes them much pain. Wanting approval from someone whose behavior you do not approve of is a true mixed message. Breaking free of the "approval trap" is crucial to recovery as an adult daughter.

Rigidity

_____ I lock myself into a course of action without serious consideration of alternate choices or consequences.

_____ I seek tension and crisis and then complain.

_____ I avoid conflict or aggravate it, but rarely deal with it.

When things go wrong, do you find the best solution or do you accept the first solution? Do you apply the same strategies for handling all problems? Many adult daughters unfortunately believe that they inherited the same problem-solving skills that were used in their families. If you believe this, you are locked into a pattern of rigidity that is difficult to break.

For example, how good are you in a crisis? Many adult daughters state that they are more comfortable in a crisis than in everyday living situations. Have you become accustomed to living on the emotional edge? When you are in "normal" situations, do you find yourself waiting for something to go wrong? Additionally, if something does go wrong, do you find yourself unable to stop discussing it? You may be locked into rigid patterns and not know it. You are probably doing what you know best and are most comfortable doing, but these reactions are not the healthiest for you. In a dysfunctional family, having things go wrong becomes normal. Later, when you are in a truly normal situation, you are waiting for something negative to occur. Adult daughters often state that they have to learn new behaviors and break old negative patterns in order to feel comfortable and good about healthy situations and people.

Fear of Failure

_____ I fear rejection and abandonment, yet I reject others.
_____ I fear failure, but I downgrade my successes.
_____ I fear criticism and judgment, yet I criticize others.

I was always looking for that fatal flaw. I always suspected that there was something they needed from me and that they didn't really want me. . . . And eventually it would fizzle. I've been married and divorced and I've had other relationships that just haven't worked.

Nora

The characteristics in this section are two-sided. That is, you do one thing in contradiction of another. Many adult daughters who fear failure state that one of the reasons for their behaviors is that they are unsure of themselves. A characteristic that is not on this list, but which many adult daughters share, is that they have problems making their own decisions. How good are you at making decisions on your own? Do you ask everyone else what you should do? Were you criticized as a child when you made your own decisions, or were your decisions considered to be poor choices? If you fear failure, is the fear based solely on being afraid to fail or is it based on a fear that others will reject or abandon you if you fail?

Another aspect of the fear of failure is related to a fear of criticism. How well do you handle criticism? If you are criticized, do you take it so personally that you emotionally fall apart? If you are criticized, do you feel that not only are you rejected by whoever criticizes you, but also that you reject yourself?

How did you do on the above questions? Did you identify with all of them or only a few? If you identified strongly with many of the questions and found yourself frequently saying, "I do that," you are not very different from other adult daughters. In fact, adult daughters identify overall with the above characteristics 20 percent more than do women raised in nonalcoholic families. Additionally, adult daughters typically have higher scores on every one of the characteristics than do women from nonalcoholic families. (A more detailed table comparing characteristics of adult daughters is in the Appendix.)

If you identify with the above characteristics, is something wrong with you? No. Such identification can mean several things. Perhaps you are very aware and honest about your behaviors. Second, as the daughter of an alcoholic, you are very "normal" when compared to other adult daughters. Isn't it comforting to know that you belong and that you are not the only one? Third, you may be out of balance in certain areas of your life, but this condition does not make you a dysfunctional person.

For example, the most commonly identified characteristic of adult daughters is taking themselves very seriously. Do you know what women raised in nonalcoholic families identify as their most common characteristic? Taking themselves very seriously. However, the difference between you and a woman from a nonalcoholic family may be the degree to which you possess the characteristic. After all, a certain amount of seriousness is found in all adults and is part of being an adult. Therefore, you don't have to become the opposite of what you are now. You can, however, recover to a point that will allow you to achieve a balance in yourself.

Have you noticed that common among most of the above characteristics is their external focus? For example, for every characteristic that we identify with, we look outside of ourselves for the answer or we are admitting how much we are externally controlled. The more that you identify with these characteristics, the more you are identifying with others and the less you identify with yourself. Being externally focused is being out of balance. Focusing on yourself and reducing your excessive dependence on others will allow you not only to reduce the above characteristics in you, but will also help you achieve a sense of personal balance.

Another way of interpreting these scores might focus on what they mean for adult daughters who are trying to change or recover from their childhoods. Many adult children who read the list of characteristics about adult children often believe that change means eliminating all of the characteristics. However, since all adults identify to some degree with the characteristics, change does not mean eliminating the characteristics, but rather reducing them to manageable levels. You do not have to eliminate all the parts of who you are now—only the extreme and painful ones.

AFTERTHOUGHTS

If you're going to look back on something and laugh about it,
you might as well laugh about it now.

MARIE OSMOND

Keep your face to the sunshine and you cannot see the shadow.

HELEN KELLER

A woman is like a tea bag. It's only when she's in hot water
that you realize how strong she is.

NANCY REAGAN

The best protector any woman can have . . . is courage.

ELIZABETH CADY STANTON

We are falling apart inside, and that is why
we are falling apart outside.

MARIANNE WILLIAMSON

Chapter 10

What Kind of Adult Daughter Are You?

Yeah, you still hear the tapes, the old tapes, rolling in your head, and it's real uncomfortable. Because you know deep down inside you don't want to live your life like that.

Marcia

What kind of adult daughter are you today? Have you carried any of your childhood patterns into your adult life? If so, do these patterns help or hinder you now? As a child, you probably adjusted to your situation as best you could. Usually adapting to life with an alcoholic requires developing certain behaviors to adjust to the situation. Do you know what your adjustment behaviors were? Can you identify them or did they "just happen"? Most adult daughters had no great design for adjusting to an alcoholic family, but rather they utilized certain behaviors and personality characteristics in order to minimize pain and to survive their families.

As a child in your family, did you ever consider whether your adaptive behaviors were positive or negative for you? Probably not. However, if you could look outside of yourself and examine your in-home "coping strategies" as a child, you would probably assume that your behavior patterns were positive at the time. In other words, they helped you to adjust to the alcoholism in your family. In fact, according to Susan Volchok, your behavior patterns probably provided guidelines for you and helped you in several ways (1985). For example, your behavior patterns

- Kept you from being abandoned
- Provided you with guidelines for acceptable behavior
- Met the expectations of others
- Helped you to create some balance in your life
- Helped you to overcome inconsistency and chaos

Now that you are an adult, do you still use the same patterns when you interact with others, even though you are no longer in the same situation? If so, you have carried your childhood behaviors into your adulthood. Are these behaviors still positive for you? Probably not. The negative side of continuing to fulfill your patterns, according to Volchok, includes

- Keeping you from being totally yourself
- Impeding you from developing alternative behaviors
- Affecting your self-concept
- Creating pressure for you to comply with old patterns

Your patterns are likely not limited to being totally negative or totally positive, but rather they are more likely to be both. For example, you probably have behaviors that you learned in your family that still help you adjust, survive and relate to others today. Although you may have learned these skills painfully, or because you had no choice, they can still work to your benefit. On the other hand, many behaviors that helped you in a crisis are no longer needed when you are not in a crisis. If you continue to use them, they become negative or create new crises for you in your present relationships. For example, being overly in control might have helped in the alcoholic family but will surely cause problems in normal relationships for you now.

Most of your patterns developed over time during your childhood. If you continue to use them, you continue to reinforce them. They are no longer necessary, but they are now old patterns and habits. Can you break your old patterns, or are you locked in an emotional "habit cage"? Do you feel that because you once developed certain behaviors that you will always have them, or do you believe that you can change? More importantly, do you want to break free of childhood behaviors or roles? If they are holding you back and they keep you from growing, you know that they are not the patterns necessary to create a healthy you. "Will you change your patterns?" is one question, but "Are you even aware of them in yourself?" is another.

In this chapter, we discuss the patterns or typologies of adult daughters and the positive and negative attributes of each. Do you have any idea what parts of you are worth keeping and what parts you would like to change? The rest of this chapter can help you sort out these parts and patterns.

Typologies of Adult Daughters

At least eight different patterns of behaviors in adult daughters have carried over from childhood. These different patterns can help you to discover and understand yourself more fully. Wanting to change is one thing; knowing *what* you want to change is another story. How well do you know yourself and your behaviors? While you read through the different patterns, you will frequently admit, "I do that." As we discuss each pattern and its characteristics, you should keep several thoughts in mind.

1. **Each type has positive and negative implications.**

You are a survivor and therefore you have the skills to survive. You possess many positive qualities, whether you are aware of them or not. You possess many characteristics that have the potential to be used positively. On the other hand, certain characteristics in each type can cause you pain and keep you from enjoying your life. For each type of adult daughter, we identify positive and negative characteristics. The key to recovery is overcoming the negative characteristics in yourself and turning them into assets. Do you have the key? Some of you are probably saying, "The key? I'm not sure I can find the lock!"

2. Overlaps exist between the types.

No one type completely describes any adult daughter. You are more likely to identify with one or several of the types more than with others. You will probably identify with some of the parts of each type. However, most adult daughters are astute at recognizing their behaviors and which type or behaviors apply to them.

3. Not all behaviors can be "alcoholized."

Not all of your characteristics can be traced to being a daughter of an alcoholic. Other factors contribute to who you are. One of these, for example, can be your birth order in your family; certain personality characteristics are found in children depending upon their ordinal position in their families. For example, the oldest or the firstborn often possesses such characteristics as being self-assured, a responsible high achiever, needy of recognition from others, and one who focuses on semantics and responds to problems analytically.

If you are the second child, some of your characteristics might be insecurity until you know where you fit, the ability to detect the emotional needs of others, and the capacity to be a good listener, but perhaps emotionally distant.

Third-born children are usually comfortable with people, possess good social skills, develop in-depth relationships slowly, find it difficult to separate from relationships and withdraw during conflict until they find a solution.

The fourth child in a family is usually outgoing, adventuresome and less ambitious, as well as being impulsive and demonstrative with feelings. The fourth child usually makes friends easily and takes on the stress of others to relieve tension in a relationship.

Researchers indicate that the characteristics begin to repeat themselves beginning with the fifth child. Thus, the fifth child would have the characteristics of the first and the sixth child would have those of the second, and so on (Hoopes, 1987).

As we examine each type of adult daughter, we discuss how patterns developed in her alcoholic family. You, however, can add to your understanding of each type by considering how your birth order may have influenced how you adjusted. When we account for birth order and gender development, we should find some of the same characteristics both in adult daughters and women from the healthiest families. Not everything can be attributed to alcoholism.

4. Patterns can be changed.

Your patterns and characteristics can be changed, altered or abandoned. For each type, we discuss the transitions needed to change what may be liabilities from your past into your future assets.

Are you ready to find yourself? Let's begin.

The Achiever

"Ladies and gentlemen: Presenting the all-knowing, ever competent, totally in control, most responsible woman in the world, and perfect adult daughter!" Does this sound like your introduction to the world? Are you playing the part well (perfectly)? The role looks good to others, doesn't it? How does it look to you? How does it feel?

The achieving adult daughter is accomplishment-oriented. If this description fits you, you know the pattern well. You are recognized through your accomplishments. You believe that if your behavior is worth something, then you are worth something. The problem with this kind of thinking is that your worth is always external. Other people hold your validation, and the only way to be validated is to do things that others recognize as worthwhile.

Receiving some validation is usually not a problem for you because you are extremely competent and skilled. Your problems come because you realize that you cannot validate yourself internally. The emotional motivation behind most achieving adult daughters is a sense of inadequacy or not being good enough. How many times do we hear from adult daughters that whatever they do is not good enough? How do they respond to this? They try harder. Not being good enough can also mean that you feel you are not as good as other people. Deep down inside, you feel that others are always better than you and you are constantly trying to prove yourself, but to whom: them or you?

As you might suspect, perfectionism is a classic characteristic of the achiever. For example, if you think that something is okay or done correctly, does it have to be 100 percent correct? On the other hand, does it only take a 1 percent error for the entire thing to be wrong?

> I'm my worst enemy when it comes to beating myself up. I can do it without any help from anybody. If I had done it this way instead of the way I did, it would have been better. But I did it this way and I made a mistake, I got caught and the whole world is going to fall in on top of me because I made a mistake. So I try hard not to make mistakes in my job, my home and in relationships.
>
> *Mary Carol*

In relationships, the achiever wants to be in control and is usually willing to do more than her share to achieve it. If you are an achiever, do you usually intellectualize rather than express your feelings? Do you have an image of what a "perfect relationship" should be, but rarely find one to live up to your expectations? When you have relationship problems, rather than dealing with them you will do what you do best, such as work harder. This approach keeps you externally focused. You keep people at an emotional distance and rarely have your needs met as a result of keeping others away. All of these behaviors allow you to feel in control and safe. However, do they allow you to have the kind of relationships that you would like?

Adult-daughter achievers have so much going for them because of their skills and competencies. With a little adjustment and developing the ability to validate themselves internally for being a healthy person as opposed to what they do now, they can recover well. Remember, recovering well does not mean recovering perfectly.

The potential positive and leftover negative patterns of the achiever are as follows:

Positive	Negative
Competent	Overly competitive
Good in a crisis	Perfectionist
Reliable	Difficulty relaxing
Meets goals	Fails to take care of self
Powerful and in control	Can't express feelings
Successful	Externally validated only
Survivor	Workaholic
Motivates self and others	Never wrong
	Marries a dependent person
	Compulsive
	Fears failure
	Unable to play

Transitions needed for the adult-daughter achiever in recovery are:

- Develop an internal sense of validation in yourself.
- Learn to say "no" to others and yourself.
- Find time for yourself.
- Learn to relax and slow down.
- Learn to appreciate yourself.

The Triangulator

The adult daughter who is a triangulator never deals with anyone or anything directly. If you do this, chances are that when something goes wrong for you, you are more likely to find an outside reason or excuse rather than to look at yourself. For example, you end up in trouble and you blame it on the weather. You might be having a problem in a relationship, but rather than deal with it directly, you put off dealing with the problem because you fear it might upset someone else. Most triangulators are typically noticed when they have trouble or conduct disorders, or they develop relationship problems, but they will not focus on any issue directly.

Adult-daughter triangulators probably learned their behaviors from their parents' relationship. The adult daughter may have been used as the focal point between the parents because they did not want to deal directly with each other either. Therefore, they used their daughter as an excuse or an external focus point not to deal with their own problems. Did this happen to you, and are you repeating the pattern?

Fifteen years ago I was blaming my mother for ruining my life. I would have never married that jerk if it weren't for her getting divorced, marrying my stepdad and making my life so miserable that I had to move out. I blamed her for that, and I was very angry with her.

Gloria

Often the emotional motivations behind triangulating are anger, resentment, hurt and a fear of abandonment. These emotions often lead the adult daughter into inappropriate behaviors, which she is now held responsible for, but which she would like to blame on others. The triangulator is closely associated to Lee Ann Hoff's idea that some people in a crisis react by channeling their emotions into negative behaviors.

> As a kid I could be real angry, and I would be sent to my room. I would sit there and smolder and just be angry. Now I'm trying to learn what's beneath the anger and work through it. Generally, it's fear and loneliness. It's fear of rejection, fear of abandonment or fear of being hurt.
>
> *Adele*

Few adult daughters fall into this triangulation pattern, but those who do are likely to have certain relationship problems. Do you deal with the relationship problems or blame the other person? Do you find yourself always manipulating to get what you want? Has your relationship partner accused you of being irresponsible and not contributing your share to the relationship? Do you find being close to someone difficult because you believe that no one understands you? Both positive and negative characteristics could emerge from this triangulator pattern:

Positive	**Negative**
Creative	Conduct disorders
Courageous	Poor communication skills
Good under pressure	Blames world for problems
Lots of friends	Manipulative
Commands attention	Angry
Adventuresome	Irresponsible
	Substance abuser
	Passive-aggressive

Transitions needed for the adult-daughter triangulator in recovery are:

- Learn to accept responsibility for your behaviors.
- Learn appropriate ways to handle or release anger.
- Learn how to communicate directly.
- Learn alternative ways to handle stress.

The Passive One

If you are a passive adult daughter, your patterns are difficult to assess. Unlike some of the other patterns, what you are doing is not what makes you noticed; rather, what you are *not* doing classifies you. While adult daughters who display some of the other typologies are characterized by their actions and what they are doing, passive adult daughters can be recognized by what is being done to them or how they usually just go along with everything. They are never players in the game, but always spectators. They are never actors, but reactors. Their unspoken motto of passivity implies that "life is a rehearsal."

Do you have a low opinion of yourself or feel that your needs are not as important as those of others? Do you too often go along to get along? Do you often feel that if others knew all about you they wouldn't like you? If so, you have some of the passive adult daughter characteristics. Your emotional motivations as a passive adult daughter are that you feel unimportant, what you want doesn't count and you usually feel hopeless in a crisis.

With low self-esteem, I constantly cast myself in the master-servant relationship role. Giving, giving, giving until you have nothing left for your own development and growth. I only felt satisfaction when everyone else around me was happy and content.

I completely suffocated my own needs and feelings. . . . The voice of denial nags at me, saying, "Your life was full of opportunities. It's not that bad." I had no identity and therefore became an appendage of my husband.

Jeannie

In relationships, passive adult daughters are likely to tolerate a tremendous amount of inappropriate behavior, are always willing to be second and seldom express their needs. If conflicts develop, passive adult daughters are likely to take the path of least resistance, which usually means to do what the other person wants. Passive adult daughters internalize relationship problems, but will not discuss them for fear of abandonment. Additionally, they are at added risk for developing eating disorders.

Passive adult daughter characteristics include the following:

Positive	Negative
Tolerant	Won't stand up for self
Willing to help others	Low self-worth
Highly adaptable	Always puts others first
Loyal friends	Lonely
Independent	Fears reality
Good listener	Depressed
Empathic	Joyless
	Used in relationships
	Eating disorders
	Confused
	Shy

Transitions needed for passive adult daughters in recovery are:

• Learn to take care of yourself first.
• Do things to raise your self-esteem.

- Learn to feel good about yourself.
- Learn to accept being liked by others.
- Stop doing what you do not do; take action.

The Other-Directed One

Adult daughters who are other-directed rely heavily on others' opinions of what they should do, hide their feelings by displaying the exact opposite of their emotions, and feel as if their lives are out of control. If you are an other-directed adult daughter, do you believe that you must portray the exact opposite of how you feel? Why would you do this? Usually you feel that if you do not portray the opposite, others will reject you or abandon you. The emotional motivation for allowing yourself to be other-directed is deeply rooted in a fear of exposing your feelings and your needs . . . a fear of being abandoned.

I found that I grew up with a fear that my father was going to leave. It was a fear of abandonment and losing somebody important. I realized that I brought my fear into my marriage. It's like from the day we got married, subconsciously thinking, *I know he's going to leave me. He's not going to love me enough to stay.* I started building up defenses and at the same time trying to do everything he wanted to keep him from leaving. So far, he's still here.

Denise

The adult daughter who is other-directed believes that to be accepted she should do what others want her to do. If she is in pain, she will hide it because she believes that pain is unacceptable to others. Usually you will hide your pain by displaying the exact opposite of how you feel. After all, if you pretend that you are happy, no one will notice your turmoil, or so you believe.

Do you often feel as if you are "programmed"? For example, do you feel that you must constantly meet everyone else's expectations, but never your own? When you are other-directed, you become externally focused. You often say to yourself, *I feel like I do everything for everyone else, but I never do anything for myself.* Other-directed adult daughters have a limited sense of self-identity and identity boundary problems. For example, they are not sure where their identity ends and another person's begins because they overly identify with what the other person thinks they should do. The other-directed adult daughter looks into the mirror and sees a reflection of herself not as she sees herself, but as she believes other people see her.

If you are an other-directed adult daughter, how do you respond in relationships? Do you have difficulty making decisions in a relationship? Do you constantly defer to the other person by saying, "Whatever you want, I want"? Do you feel that you are behaviorally stuck in your relationships? In other words, you cannot behave the way you would like and you are limited to only those behaviors that your partner approves. Additionally, are your relationships characterized by being overly sensitive to criticism, denial of your own feelings and difficulty establishing your boundaries?

The positive and negative characteristics of the other-directed adult daughter include:

Positive	Negative
Attracts attention	Overly controlled by others
Charming	Tense, anxious
Sense of humor	Overreactive
Can anticipate needs	Shallow relationships

Positive	Negative
Adaptable	Indecisive
Team player	No sense of self
Cooperative	Overly dependent
Joyful	Needs to please others only
Energetic	Needs constant approval
	Poor sense of boundaries

Transitions needed for other-directed adult daughters in recovery are:

- Learn to develop a sense of what is right for you.
- Stop being controlled by others.
- Learn to express your needs and ideas.
- Establish your own sense of self and boundaries.
- Start doing what you want to do.

The Conflict Avoider

I tend to be a people-pleaser, a "Red Crosser." I look for people I can help and rescue. I used to thrive on chaos and challenges, but I am learning to love calmness, order and quietness in my life. Learning to love myself is a very big problem. I had to learn to get my hands off everything in the lives of my husband and children.

Stephanie

Do you find yourself in the middle of everyone else's problems? Are you willing to help everyone else with his or her problems, but avoid your own? If so, you may be a conflict-avoider adult daughter. This type of adult daughter appears willing to help others. She is the neighborhood counselor and the person who others rely on for solutions. The irony is that this adult daughter wants to avoid conflicts in her life more than anything else. Why then does she help other people with their problems? Because they are other people's problems and thus she can avoid facing her own. For example, she might be thinking, *The more I am willing to help you, and my cousins, and my neighbors and so on, the more I can keep you away from me and the less I have to face my own problems.*

The emotional motivation for the conflict avoider is a fear of arguments and personal conflict. She will do anything to avoid an argument, whether hers or someone else's. Therefore, if you are a conflict avoider, you likely engage in a lot of people-pleasing behaviors. The conflict avoider does not think that healthy arguments exist. All arguments are to be avoided. However, she can spot trouble before it occurs because she is very sensitive to the warning signs. How does she respond when she sees trouble coming? She pulls out her box of "emotional Band-Aids" and applies them before the wounds become too deep. However, this approach usually leads to postponing problems, denying the real issues involved and never having anything resolved.

In relationships, the conflict-avoider adult daughter is highly vulnerable to being used. She will disproportionately focus on the problems of the other person and will do almost anything to keep arguments from occurring in her relationships. Ironically, she hates arguments, but when they occur she feels that her responsibility is to resolve them. How does she resolve them? By minimizing their existence, denial or avoiding the necessary steps involved for resolution. In her relationships, she often feels that she is constantly placating others and usually has a low self-worth. She suffers from a "justifiable negative attention" image of herself. For example, she believes that the only time she can receive emotional support from others is when something beyond her control has happened to her, such as an accident or an illness. Then receiving attention is okay. This approach puts her at great risk for having to manipulate others in order to acquire what she wants or needs. She does not feel good about herself and thus has difficulty accepting good feelings about herself from others.

Some of the positive and negative characteristics of the conflict avoider are as follows:

Positive	Negative
Willing to help others	Unrealistic opinion of arguments
Good in a crisis	Constantly placating others
Good negotiator	Powerlessness
Problem solver	Depression
Persistent	Denial
Sensitive to others	Takes on too many problems
Thinks of alternatives	Seldom happy
Good communicator	Intimidated
	Inability to receive
	User relationships

Transitions needed for conflict-avoider adult daughters in recovery are:

- Recognize and focus on your own problems.
- Quit taking on the problems of others.
- Learn to accept positive attention.
- Learn the difference between helping someone and feeling responsible for their problems and solutions.
- Be willing to receive help from others.

The Hypermature

Do you take yourself very seriously? Are you always emotionally on guard? Do you find letting yourself go or genuinely having fun difficult? Have you always felt that you were more mature than your peers? If so, chances are that you identify very strongly with the hypermature adult daughter pattern.

> I took my role too seriously. I tried too hard to keep my sons away from drugs and alcohol. I was an either/or person with no room for gray areas. I tried to make my children achieve too much and grow up too soon. I loved them through their accomplishments and lived vicariously through their lives. I centered all of my energies on my children and ignored my husband.
>
> *Cleo*

Hypermaturity differs from the other patterns by indicating more about one's attitudes than about behaviors. Most of the other patterns focus on the various behavioral patterns associated with each type of adult daughter. The hypermature adult daughter, however, thinks of herself differently, being very reserved and striving to maintain total control over her emotions. The motivation for hypermaturity is to be emotionally on guard and always prepared.

If you are a hypermature adult daughter, not only do you take yourself very seriously, but you also take everything that you do very seriously. You are the "eternal parent" in the group. You are the one who always thinks of everything that could go wrong and then you plan accordingly. Your ability to anticipate other people's actions is uncanny. You are highly reliable, but you have a great deal of difficulty allowing anyone to do anything for you. Besides, you probably believe they could not do it as good as you can. Additionally, people who do not take things as seriously as you do may irritate you.

Some of the most common problems that we find in hypermature adult daughters is that they have a general feeling of being "burned out" and that something is missing in their lives. Usually, they began their lives as adults too early. For example, they took on tremendous responsibilities in early adolescence, and the emotional overload is beginning to catch up with them. They never had time to be a child. "When I was young, I was never a child" is a common statement of the hypermature adult daughter. They have a difficult time acting their age, even as adults. After all, no one said that we cannot have joy and laughter in our lives now, or that the joy of being a child must be limited to the childhood years. The healthiest people are "age androgynous." That is, healthy individuals possess the best aspects of being young and an adult at the same time. One of the best indicators of recovery is developing a healthy sense of humor. The hypermature adult daughter often confuses intellectual sarcasm with humor. Laughter, warmth and time for yourself should be part of every stage of your life, so remember to act your age!

If you are a hypermature adult daughter, how does this affect your relationships? Typically, you are extreme in most of the things that you do, including your relationships. You find it difficult to take relationships lightly and you make everything too intense. You often hear from your relationship person that you are too serious: "Lighten up, will you?" You allow yourself to feel that you are disproportionately responsible for the success of a relationship. If the relationship fails, you will judge yourself without mercy. Fun is often missing in your relationships and, even when you do take time for yourself, you are constantly analyzing everything or you are worrying about all of the things that you have to do. Most of the time you are at risk for feeling overwhelmed and emotionally drained in your relationships.

If the hypermature adult daughter can learn to take life easy and not take herself and everything about herself so seriously, then she can change her negative characteristics into assets. The positive and negative characteristics for the hypermature adult daughter include the following:

Positive	Negative
Organized	Too serious
Analytical	Difficulty expressing emotions
Prepared	Constantly needing control
Mature	Stress-related illnesses
Reliable	Not much fun
Intuitive	Fearful
Meets goals	Driven
Attentive	Avoids taking risks
	Critical
	Blames self too much

Transitions needed for the hypermature adult daughter in recovery are:

- Learn to relax and have fun.
- Let others take charge.
- Allow yourself to express emotions.
- Adjust your priorities to reduce feeling overwhelmed.
- Laugh more.

The Detacher

The adult daughter who is a detacher wants to remove herself emotionally and psychologically from all situations that she feels are undesirable. This pattern usually starts in adolescence when she decides that although she must live with her dysfunctional family, it "isn't going to bother me anymore." Therefore, such adult daughters tried to emotionally detach from the situation, and as soon as they were able to physically leave, they were gone. The assumption was, *All*

I have to do is leave, and I will leave all of this behind.

Knowing when to detach yourself from an unhealthy situation can be a healthy response. The kind of detachment that can cause problems for you is based on what is called premature closure. Premature closure occurs when you are not willing to deal with anything or anyone that makes you uncomfortable, and your first response is to leave. This approach does not allow you the opportunity to work things out or to find solutions. The same response begins to be employed in all problem situations: You want to leave. The emotional motivation for the adult-daughter detacher is to avoid being hurt. She will attempt to avoid hurt by trying to become nonfeeling or emotionally numb.

Do you pretend that nothing bothers you? Do you believe that you can emotionally separate yourself from situations that you don't like? Do you look for solutions in your relationships, or when something first goes wrong do you want to end it? Do you deny unpleasant events? If so, you might be detaching and not allowing yourself the opportunity for resolution or expressing feelings. After all, when you physically detach, you believe that you can emotionally detach as well, which is where the problem lies for most detaching adult daughters. For example, they believe that they have successfully detached from their alcoholic family, but don't bring up the situation! If your detaching kept you from being involved emotionally, why such strong emotions? The truth is that most detachers do not detach, but use this pattern as a way to avoid dealing with the emotional baggage that they want to deny exists. This kind of thinking and behavior traps you emotionally. If you detached successfully, you would have no emotions from your past, but if the feelings persist, doesn't that mean that your detaching wasn't successful?

As you might suspect, if you are a detaching adult daughter, you will be very hard to reach. You believe that by detaching you have protected yourself. You believe that if you *don't* detach, you will be vulnerable and not in control of your emotions. Therefore, in order to work on your issues, you will need to accept that some things have affected you and that your emotions are not resolved. You will need to confront a very intimidated person: yourself.

In relationships, the adult-daughter detacher wants to flee immediately any uncomfortable situation. If she even senses that trouble is coming, she is likely to want out. On the other hand, her perception of what constitutes a healthy relationship is not realistic. To her, a "good" relationship is totally trouble-free. Therefore, she will likely proceed to jump from one relationship to another, either looking for the good one or leaving the existing one early because she senses problems coming. Always detaching has denied her the skills to resolve relationship conflict. Her opinion of relationship problems is that the other person causes them. Consider a detacher who has had six relationships with men, all six of which collapsed. What does she deduce from her experiences? Something is wrong with men, and the same thing is wrong with every one of them. Now in her seventh relationship, the same problems arise again. A typical response for the detacher would be, "Look, if you're having problems with this relationship, they are your problems. If you can't handle it, I'm out of here."

Maybe you're thinking that you've waited years to tell that to some guy, but think about what the detacher has denied herself. She denies herself developing the kinds of skills that will help in relationships. She denies her own feelings, and she denies learning a healthy concept of what makes a good relationship. She becomes detached from her own needs.

My biggest problem was not liking myself. I never believed others really liked or loved me, and I was always suspicious of their motives. I have a fear of anger in myself and in others. I lack trust. I always have a wall between myself and others to assure that I don't get hurt.

Grace

The positive and negative characteristics of the adult-daughter detacher include the following:

Positive	Negative
Perceptive	Rigid attitudes
Sets limits	Jealous, suspicious
Can spot trouble	Defiant
Independent	Lonely
Self-motivated	Nonfeeling
Traveler	High risk for addiction
Nonconformist	Secretive
	Inner anger
	Fears being hurt
	Denial

Transitions needed for the adult-daughter detacher in recovery are:

- Learn interpersonal relationship skills.
- Develop a realistic concept of healthy relationships.
- Develop alternatives for handling stress.
- Learn to identify and express your emotions.
- Learn to accept help and support from others.

The Invulnerable

Do any healthy adult daughters exist? Absolutely! Consider the invulnerable adult daughter. Many studies have found that some children who are raised in extremely dysfunctional families emerge as very healthy adults (Garmezy, 1976; Werner, 1986).

That everyone describes adult children consistently in only negative terms is a mystery. Where do the healthy ones belong, or what about the healthy parts that are found in all adult children? The invulnerable pattern can develop in adult daughters in three ways. One way is when the adult daughter, without any formal intervention, emerges as a healthy adult. The second form occurs when the adult daughter is able to work through many of her issues and feelings. Through her personal recovery, she becomes an invulnerable. The third way occurs when the adult daughter begins to recognize and accept those parts of her that are healthy and competent. Parts of you are invulnerable. We could identify positive characteristics in each of the previous seven patterns because parts of you *are* positive. More importantly, you have the ability to grow even further.

What does "invulnerable" mean? That nothing affects you and that you are indestructible? No. The true invulnerable adult daughter is one who does not deny her feelings, her experiences or her pain. However, she accepts all of her feelings and experiences; when she is feeling vulnerable, she will not only admit it but will ask for and accept help. Many of the other typologies will deny their feelings when they need help and thus deny help. The invulnerable adult daughter does not deny, but accepts and then acts to maintain her own health.

How well do you care for your emotional self? Are you willing to allow yourself to admit when you are vulnerable? Do you ever ask for help and allow yourself to receive it? Can you identify your invulnerable traits? Are you turning your childhood liabilities into adult characteristics that will work well for you?

Invulnerables are made, not born. You become invulnerable

through your actions and your attitudes. You learn to use the positive traits that have been identified in all adult daughters. You learn that you have never lost your abilities to hope, to risk, to try, to forgive, to grow beyond your injuries, to share, to love and to recognize that you are a good person.

In relationships, invulnerable adult daughters know how to achieve balance. If you are an invulnerable adult daughter, your relationships are typically healthy. You know how to give and receive. Your emotional and physical needs are being met. You are able to express your needs, and you are able to negotiate openly with your partner. You can be yourself without fearing rejection, and you are loved for who you are. Additionally, you are a great partner in a relationship. Your health is obvious and contagious.

Since the invulnerable presents quite differently than the other patterns, knowing some characteristics found in invulnerable adult daughters would be helpful. Transitions aren't needed in the same way as for the other typologies, because the invulnerable adult daughter is always growing. How many of the following invulnerable behaviors do you have?

- You know how to attract and use the support of those who are around you.
- You have developed a healthy sense of humor.
- You have developed a well-balanced sense of autonomy.
- You are socially at ease and others are comfortable around you.
- You are willing to identify and express your feelings.
- You can work through your problems.
- You are neither controlled nor controlling.
- You do not live in fear of your past, but with the joy of the present.
- You like yourself.

Today I love myself. Today I am real special. . . . I see myself like a rose, or better yet, when you plant a garden you plant a seed. A seed has been planted in me, and it's growing into a flower, a flower that's blossoming. As it opens, doors open in my life. For each door that opens, there's a new experience. From that experience I find inner peace and self-love that we all deserve. I sure do . . . today. I'm okay, I'm real okay.

Lillian

AFTERTHOUGHTS

*Let the world know you as you are, not as you think you should
be, because sooner or later, if you are posing,
you will forget the pose, and then where are you?*

FANNY BRICE

*It's usually the most wounded among us
who inflict pain on others.*

PATTI DAVIS

*Life's challenges are not supposed to paralyze you;
they're supposed to help you discover who you are.*

BERNICE JOHNSON REAGON

Deep down I'm pretty superficial.

AVA GARDNER

*A bad habit never disappears miraculously;
it's an undo-it-yourself project.*

ABIGAIL VAN BUREN

Chapter 11

I'm Not
Codependent, Are We?

Do you find yourself using old solutions to new problems and they don't work? Are you torn between your old patterns of behavior and a conscious awareness to want to change, but you don't know how? Do you know what is holding you back and keeping you from growing? Are you afraid to be yourself, especially in relationships? If these questions apply to you, you have many "leftovers" from childhood that lead you into patterns of unhealthy behaviors. These patterns can lead to codependency.

> Yeah, you're always looking over your shoulder waiting for the cloud, right?
>
> *Melissa*

Codependency has many definitions. Its origins trace back to assessing how nonalcoholic family members are affected not just by someone else's alcoholism, but by exposure to life in a dysfunctional family. Even codependency cannot be totally alcoholized. Robert Subby defines codependency as "an emotional, psychological and behavioral condition that develops as a result of an individual's prolonged exposure to, and practice of, a set of oppressive rules—rules which prevent the open expression of feeling, as well as the direct discussion of personal and interpersonal problems" (1987).

Did you grow up in a family that was not only alcoholic, but also had many spoken and unspoken oppressive rules? No one ever voted on these rules, but they were maintained nonetheless. Did you feel at times that you were living life in an emotional dictatorship? Do you still feel out of balance as a result of your experiences?

> It's difficult to put values, trust and love all back together again because what you thought it was, isn't there anymore. So we were always raised to be very independent. It's very difficult for

me to allow others in to see what is going on inside. . . . It's a difficult life being the independent person, trying to make everything work the way you think it should work, and putting the pieces together.

Wendy

Think about the previous chapter on behavior patterns in adult daughters. If you disproportionately identified with the negative characteristics and found most of your behaviors in the negative column, you probably have many codependent behaviors. Codependency causes you to be out of balance emotionally and behaviorally in your life. Codependency keeps you externally focused and does not allow you to develop a healthy sense of self that can lead to a well-balanced life.

Like everything else that we have discussed, your codependency is dependent upon the degree to which your alcoholic family has affected you. When you are out of balance, you are either too much one way or the other—for example, giving too much in one situation and not enough in another. All adult daughters can display some characteristics that could identify with codependency, but occasional displays do not make one codependent. The *degree* to which these characteristics exist determines codependency. If many of your behaviors are causing you pain, and you are obviously stuck in your old patterns, you will probably identify heavily with the characteristics of codependency.

High-Risk Characteristics for Codependency

Are you codependent? Could you become codependent? What are the characteristics, and are you at risk for developing them? How much do you identify with the following statements?

- I have an overdeveloped/underdeveloped sense of responsibility, and being concerned with others is easier, even if I ignore my own legitimate needs.
- I "stuff" my feelings about my own childhood, and I have lost the ability to feel or express feelings because doing so hurts too much.
- I am physically or emotionally isolated from and afraid of people and authority figures.
- I have become addicted to approval or excitement, and I have lost my identity in the process.
- Angry people and personal criticism frighten me.
- I live as a victim.
- I judge myself harshly, and I have low self-esteem.
- I am very dependent and terrified of abandonment. I will hold on to any relationship to keep from being abandoned.
- I experience guilt feelings when I stand up for myself.
- I have become chemically dependent or am a compulsive undereater or overeater, or I have found another compulsive personality person, such as a workaholic, to fulfill my compulsive needs.

The above behaviors, if practiced too much, would put you at a high risk for codependency. When we consider codependency, however, I believe that we must be cautious not to jump to conclusions and label too many behaviors as codependent. For example, you may have noticed that many of the behaviors associated with codependency focus on caring, thinking of others, helping in a crisis, needing approval from others and perceiving your life in relationship to others. What is wrong with these behaviors in and of themselves? Aren't these the kinds of qualities that we would like to have in ourselves and in our friends? The real question becomes, what is the line between being a warm, loving and caring person and being codependent? If we go too far in saying that any of your behaviors that support someone else are codependent, are we saying that you are wrong to care about another person?

Even codependency itself must be assessed from a position of balance. Recently, the tendency has been to define codependency too vaguely and too broadly, resulting in the inclusion of almost all nurturing behaviors. Some authors state that 96 percent of American families are codependent! That makes codependency normal, doesn't it? What are the other 4 percent of families? When the definition of codependency becomes too vague, we become vulnerable to unjustifiable conviction.

If you want to know whether or not you suffer from codependency or are at a high risk for developing it, you must assess honestly your behaviors and your emotional motivations. To accept too broad a definition might mean that you believe you must become the exact opposite of a codependent person in order to recover. You might not want to become so independent that you need absolutely no one, or that helping someone indicates how ill you are. Remember that the idea is to look for balance, not absolutes. If we become too absolute in our willingness to embrace codependency as an "explains all behaviors" phenomenon, I believe that we will be out of balance in our understanding of codependency itself.

Codependent Relationships

How do you know if you are out of balance in your life? Let's examine how you respond in your relationships. As an adult daughter, are you a healthy, warm and loving person, or are you codependent and trying to hide it by becoming warm and loving for everyone else? One of the best indicators of whether or not you are codependent hinges on how much your needs are being met. On the other hand, if you are a very giving person and your needs are still genuinely being met, you are not giving too much and you are not out of balance.

For example, Robin Norwood, in her book *Women Who Love Too Much* (1985), talks about the problem of loving too much, especially for women who were raised in dysfunctional families. Is the real problem loving too much or not being loved enough? She tells us that many women who do not feel loved and whose needs are not being met fall into the trap of trying to give what they hope to receive. Thus, by giving love away, you hope to reap it in return. What happens to you, however, if you give tremendous amounts away and have little returned? If you continue in this pattern of constantly giving more than you receive, you are locked into a codependent relationship. In a healthy relationship, your needs as well as the other person's needs should be met. In a codependent relationship, only one person's needs are being met, and unfortunately at the expense of deferring the other's needs.

> Without realizing it, I wound up picking very needy men. I played the big sister role, and I wasn't able to share feelings because I was always looking to be a better person. If I was good enough, then maybe he would be happy. I really re-created the role I played with my father. Naturally, it didn't work.
>
> *Maureen*

If you are a "good" codependent, you are good at meeting other people's needs and lousy at meeting your own. If you want to be healthy and have your needs met, you have to give up being a "good" codependent. Do you engage in any codependent behaviors in your relationships? Ask yourself if you identify with the following characteristics of codependent relationships.

- I will do almost anything to keep my relationship from falling apart because I don't want to be alone.
- I believe there is no such thing as too much effort or time that I am willing to give in my relationship so that I can help the other person.
- I never had much love in any of my relationships, so I don't expect much now.
- I try as hard as I can all the time to please the other person in my relationship. I am intimidated if they are angry.
- I often become a caregiver to needy people, but I have difficulty receiving nurturing from others.
- I keep being in relationships with people who I think I can change, or I keep hoping that they will change because they love me.
- I usually do more than my share in a relationship, and for some reason I continue doing it.
- I never feel that I am as good as the person with whom I am in a relationship.
- I want to be in control in my relationships, but I often find myself being controlled. I react to this situation by becoming more controlling.
- If my relationship has problems, I still prefer to think of how it could be, rather than how it is.
- I am in love with being "in love."
- I am always in relationships with people who are "therapy projects," and I am usually emotionally hurt while I try to fix them.
- I become depressed easily in my relationships, especially if everything is not going well.

- I am not sure that I can be comfortable or that I can remain in a healthy relationship for a long time.

For every "yes" that you answered to these questions, you said "no" to yourself. How much your childhood has affected you, how many negative patterns you have carried into your adulthood and how successfully you can recover depend upon how codependent you are. While codependency can be described in many ways, one certainty is that codependency will keep you from recovering and from becoming as healthy as you want to be.

Adult daughters who are having many problems in their lives are also the ones trapped in codependency. Codependency can surface in your relationships, your parenting skills, your self-esteem and your attempts to recover. If you are not sure that you possess any codependent characteristics, let's break it down into other behaviors and see how much you identify with them. After all, a "good" codependent is not likely to be aware of her behaviors.

When you are constantly focused on others, you have little time for your own needs. Breaking the cycle of codependency begins with discovering that you have some of the patterns. Realizing your codependency does not make you a bad person, nor should you consider yourself naive for not knowing about it. You probably did what made the most sense for you in your childhood. This "child sense" helped you to survive your alcoholic household. Now, the patterns are "nonsense," and they keep you from growing. These patterns no longer fit and cause you pain. To break the patterns, however, you have to know them. Are you maintaining any of the following patterns?

Progressive Defeat

Do you feel despair or hopelessness about changing yourself or your current situation? Have you exchanged your attitude of hope for one of pessimism? If so, you are developing an attitude of progressive defeat, an indicator of codependency. Even when you do well, do you feel good about it or do you still have a low self-esteem that does not accurately reflect your accomplishments?

Living in Fear

Living in fear can happen in many ways for adult daughters. For example, perhaps you are preoccupied with the problems of others, or you can't make claims for yourself or your own needs. Other symptoms of living in fear include being overly responsible, manipulating others' behaviors, persistent anxiety and feelings of dread. Do you fear the future? Are you often afraid that things will not improve for you? Do you fear that you are stuck in your life and that you will never learn how to break the patterns that hold you? These signs of living in fear play a major role in codependency.

Impaired Identity

As we've mentioned, your identity can be fragmented because of your alcoholic family. Loss of identity and difficulty in boundary separation from others play a major part in keeping you codependent. When you need others to always validate who you are and your worth, you suffer from impaired identity development. Not being able to separate from others and to establish your own identity keeps you at a high risk for codependency. When you are codependent, your life is never your own. Your life belongs to someone else, but you may never realize this because you are too busy identifying with that other person.

Codependency is a trap. The core of codependency is giving up your own identity. The more you are codependent, the more you identify with someone else. The more you identify with that other person, the less you think of yourself. Unfortunately, the person you disproportionately identify with will not help you break free. They selfishly will allow you to support them at the expense of sacrificing yourself. But the time has come to declare: no more human sacrifices!

Shame

Adult daughters often mentioned shame as a problem, and shame takes many different forms. For some adult daughters, shame is associated with feeling guilty about not only their behaviors, but also about others' behaviors. Shame can be the reason for wanting to minimize and deny family problems, especially alcoholism.

The most painful form of shame for adult daughters is reflected in statements of self-hatred or condemnation. Statements such as "I'm no good," "I can't do anything right," "I never please anyone" or "I'm not as good as other people" are all examples of how shame can dominate your identity and foster codependency.

Confusion

Are you often surprised to find out that your perceptions of reality or normalcy are totally wrong? Codependency can keep you not only separated from yourself, but also separated from reality. After all, once you honestly see a dysfunctional situation for what it is, denying that situation becomes harder. Denial keeps you from accepting reality, which in turn keeps you confused.

Other symptoms of confusion involve being gullible—the "I'll believe anything" syndrome—and being indecisive. When we are not sure of what is real, we become vulnerable to believing everything that we are told. One of the prerequisites to being used is allowing others to control what you believe, both about them and about yourself.

Anger

The codependent person is often angry, but not sure at what or whom. What do you do with your anger? Do you express it or keep it inside? Do you handle it directly, or do you redirect it toward someone or some activity to cover it up? Redirecting your anger is a codependent behavior.

Some adult daughters stated that they were spiritually angry. They felt as if God had let them down, not only in childhood, but also in their adult lives.

Another form of anger is unidentified anger. Do you ever find yourself walking around and feeling that you are angry for no apparent reason, but you just feel ticked off? Such free-floating anger should be a sign to you that something is wrong. The problem now is finding out what. Anger that is not released or confronted does not dissolve. Not only does such anger stay, but it continues to grow. Codependency might redirect your anger, but doesn't release it.

If you identified strongly with at least four of the above patterns, you are at high risk for codependency. Codependent adult daughters consistently shared that they felt stuck in a pattern that does not allow them to change. On the other hand, as they have become more aware of their codependency, they have become aware that their codependency impedes their recovery. The greatest consequence of codependency is that it keeps you from being yourself.

Me Phobia

Karen Blaker, in her book *Born to Please,* identifies the fear of being yourself as "me phobia" (1988). Do you often feel that you are an emotional impostor? Are you afraid of revealing the true you? Me phobia keeps you from being yourself and is especially apparent when you feel that you cannot be yourself in your relationships. Me phobia makes you feel that you must always be on guard in order to please the other person. Additionally, you are always careful not to let the real you come through. After a while you become an expert at doing what others want while simultaneously masking who you are. You become an extension of others at the expense of being separated from yourself.

Another form of me phobia is a fear of getting to know yourself. After all, what if you don't like what you find? Will you change or will you continue to fear yourself?

Me phobia and codependency were made for each other. They will live codependently ever after, but they sure won't live happily ever after. Will you? If you are at a high risk for codependency and you want to reduce your risk or alter your behaviors, you must begin with yourself. You must overcome me phobia, which may not be as difficult as you think.

Throughout this book, we have consistently stressed your positive characteristics as well as negative ones. The same principle applies to codependency. Does codependency exist? Of course. Can the term be overused and abused? Yes. Being a warm and loving person and being codependent are very different approaches to life. Overcoming me phobia may not be so difficult because many parts of you, perhaps undiscovered parts, have the potential to make you a very healthy person.

If taken to an extreme, what is the cure for codependency? Is it to display the exact opposite of all of the indicative behaviors, and what does that mean? For example, do you give up being emotional, being able to feel, being able to empathize with others, caring about other people or being compassionate? Perhaps the concept of codependency is "male-dominated" in its thinking. Overcoming codependency often seems to mean giving up behaviors and characteristics that are traditionally identified more with women than men. But codependency means being out of balance, and overcoming it does not mean giving up your potentially best qualities.

Although many of the characteristics of codependency appear to have been directed toward women, is it because women are more at risk for these behaviors? Or, have women been more willing to identify and admit when they are out of balance? Perhaps, too, male codependent behaviors have not been discovered. Can different female and male forms of codependency exist? Adult-daughter forms of codependency can develop from identifying too much with other people. Adult-son forms of codependency can develop from identifying too little with other people. Therefore, to ask adult daughters to give up all of their gender behaviors, which might be mistaken for codependency, in order to recover is the wrong approach.

If you are afraid to use your best qualities, you are still suffering from me phobia. Do not give up your qualities of being emotional, compassionate, empathic, sensitive, intimate and loving. Don't risk missing the emotional boat. Many men miss the emotional boat every day and wouldn't know a healthy relationship if they fell into one.

Use your emotional qualities to help yourself first. Keep these qualities in check when you are giving them too freely to others and remember to give them to yourself. If you give everything to everyone else and you feel used, you are codependent. If you think that you have stopped being codependent because you have totally abandoned all giving and emotional behaviors, you are now denying yourself your own emotional health. Either way, the best of you is kept from you. Give yourself a warm, loving present. Unwrap who you are, throw the wrapping away and keep your gift.

AFTERTHOUGHTS

*You can live a lifetime and, at the end of it, know more about
other people than you know about yourself.*

BERYL MARKHAM

Genuine forgiveness does not deny anger, but faces it head-on.

ALICE MILLER

So many people to rescue, so little time.

JANN MITCHELL

*The nonliberated woman and the codependent are the same
person. . . . She gets her identity completely from outside herself.*

ANNE WILSON SCHAEF

People who make some other person their job are dangerous.

DOROTHY L. SAYERS

Part Four

Concerns of the Day

Chapter 12

Relationships, or You Married a *What?*

I have no idea what a healthy relationship is, what marriage is, as far as roles, responsibilities and my rights. I give myself mixed messages. I go after someone who will take care of me, but who is emotionally unavailable. I have love-fear feelings toward sex. I am afraid of men in general. I have feelings of guilt if I follow my interests, which may differ from my partner's.

Marilyn

Are you in a relationship with a "therapy project" or did you marry one? Are you fighting for control of your relationship, or are you fighting to emerge from under someone else's control of you? Do you feel that something is missing in your relationship, but you are not sure what? On the other hand, are you in a relatively healthy relationship, but you keep waiting for it to fail or to be abandoned? Do you believe that you deserve a healthy relationship, or do you feel that you are in the relationship that you deserve? If you question your relationships and feel uncertain about them, you are like many adult daughters who stated that one of the major problems today was their relationship. In fact, relationship problems were the most frequently cited concerns for adult daughters.

In this chapter, we discuss why you are susceptible to relationship problems, the types of relationship problems that adult daughters most frequently mention, and the problem of either needing to control a relationship or being in a relationship where you are controlled. Before we proceed with the problems, though, let's start with your expectations.

What Do You Want from a Relationship?

Have you ever honestly asked yourself what you want from a relationship? Find a piece of paper, sit down and write on the top of the page, "These are my expectations and wants in a relationship." Now list what you want from a relationship. How long is your list? How aware are you of what you want? Are there differences between what you want and what you expect? The greater the differences between wants and expectations, the more likely you are to be disappointed in your relationships. Many adult daughters recognize great differences in their relationships between what they want and what they have, but they are still willing to assume most of the blame when it doesn't turn out the way they expected. In your current or past relationships with a significant or romantic other, do you or did you end up with what you wanted?

> I learned to mother men and leave them when they did not become the father I wanted. I used, abused and abandoned men, and/or I was used, abused and abandoned by men. I was sexually overactive.
>
> *Louise*

On your list of wants and expectations, how many of them are positive expectations? How many are negative? Is your list balanced, or do you expect either all positive or all negative events to occur? No relationship is all positive or all negative. However, many adult daughters share that their expectations—and in fact many of their relationships—were more negative than positive. What kinds of relationships do you have? Are they more positive than negative, or vice versa?

No matter what your expectations, one certainty is that no relationship can make up for a lost childhood. No relationship can undo the past. We cannot put those expectations on our current relationships. If you do, you will burden your relationship with unrealistic expectations. Many adult children talk about wanting to take care of the "inner child," which is that part of us that we often deny or that we were not able to experience joyfully as we were growing up. However, we must remember that this inner child is *our* inner child. Your relationship person is not responsible for treating your inner child. You are the best person to take care of your inner needs about your childhood and development. If you find someone who takes care of your inner child, you may find it initially comforting, but as you begin to grow, you will find such treatment confining and not how you want to be treated. Wanting someone to take care of the child part of you will make it very difficult for that same person to treat you as an adult.

How realistic are your expectations? Some adult daughters talk about wanting to find the perfect man and thus have very high expectations for him. Obviously, these expectations are unrealistic, too! However, if you are the perfect daughter, why not the perfect mate? These types of expectations only lead to continual disappointment. Neither you nor he ever lives up to your ideal. Should you settle for less in your relationships? Absolutely not! Many adult daughters, however, shared that because their relationships never met their expectations, they perceived that something must be wrong with them. Perhaps these adult daughters have distorted perceptions not only about what makes a good relationship, but also about what they want.

On the other hand, many adult daughters settle for less in their relationships because of their expectations and because they become trapped in controlling relationships. Low self-esteem affects your opinion about the type of relationship you think that you deserve and that you will tolerate. You could find yourself expecting very little and tolerating a lot.

What Is a Healthy Relationship?

I had a distorted perception of males. Mine was that men keep all feelings to themselves. I was lucky to marry a man not "just like my dad." But the first time he cried, I thought, *What a weak man*. He is so dependent on me. Slowly I have come to realize that my husband is not my dad.

Carmen

What is your definition of a healthy relationship? How close are your actual relationships to your definition? Do your expectations match your definition? Again, great differences can occur. You may have a good idea about a healthy relationship, but that idea does not guarantee that you will find one. More appropriately, recognizing a healthy relationship and being able to be healthy in a relationship can be two different things.

If you were writing a list of characteristics that define a healthy relationship, what would you include? Would your list include any of the following healthy relationship characteristics?

- You feel that you are respected as a person.
- Your physical and emotional needs are met.
- You like the other person, and you feel liked by them.
- You are appreciated and not taken for granted.
- You are not afraid to be yourself.
- You can communicate effectively with your partner.
- You can affirm and support one another.
- Trust, trust, trust is everywhere.
- There is a sense of humor and play.
- Responsibilities are shared.
- Your privacy is respected.
- You are not constantly fighting for control.

- You or your partner admit and seek help for your problems.
- You want to spend time together.
- Love is a verb, not a noun.
- You are growing, and the relationship is growing.
- You feel good about yourself.

Relationship Risk Factors

Are you susceptible to relationship problems? Adult daughters often feel that they are. What puts you at high risk for troubled relationships? Adult daughters do not knowingly seek out relationship problems, but many find themselves not only in a less than adequate relationship, but also not sure about what lands them in these situations.

> The old belief that I'm only loved for what I do, not for who I am . . . the fear that I'll never be good enough.
>
> *Carrie*

Several factors put adult daughters at high risk for relationship difficulties. The most obvious one is childhood in an alcoholic family. Additionally, gender socialization patterns contribute to one gender feeling more responsible for the success of a relationship than the other, as we discussed earlier.

For example, your childhood and gender patterns might put you at risk because of your life experiences. You meet a person at your lowest emotional point and you believe that "he is going to take you away from all of this." Not being taught by example because of your parents' relationship, you have very little information about what makes a healthy relationship. Often, this situation contributes to adult daughters being instantly and totally attracted to the first person who has any emotional support for them. This person usually was not the best for you, but was only the first for you.

If you were raised to think that you had to be all things in a relationship with someone else, then you were taught to expect very little, to tolerate inappropriate behaviors, to be "quiet" and to be a pleaser. These lessons put you at risk for involvement in troubled relationships.

For example, what makes some adult daughters believe that they must be people-pleasers? Being a people-pleaser puts you at risk for relationships that are out of balance, with you carrying the load. If you are a people-pleaser, chances are that you were raised to believe the following messages about yourself:

- Approval means love.
- You expect very little, but you are willing to give a lot.
- You care for others so that others will care for you.
- You become socialized to be dependent and eager to please, and you fear abandonment.
- Everyone must like you.
- Being a perfect daughter makes you feel good about yourself.
- You care for others at the expense of not caring for yourself.
- You can be invisible and caring at the same time.

If these beliefs and behaviors describe you, you are at risk for being a people-pleaser in your relationships. Most of the time you are never pleased about your own needs as a result. Most of the adult daughters who are in "pleasing him" relationships were manipulated into believing that pleasing him would bring love and security. In reality, he received what he wanted, but the adult daughter received very little in return.

Karen Blaker suggests that people-pleasing doesn't work because it makes you vulnerable to a man, you never have true approval, your capacity to accept love is limited and you lose control as a result (1988).

Another factor that puts you at a high risk for relationship problems relates to your socialization patterns. When you think of a romantic relationship, what goes through your mind? Adult daughters often mentioned excitement, romance, challenge, physical attraction and mystery. In their book *Smart Women, Foolish Choices*, Connell Cowan and Melvyn Kinder believe that many women are socialized to equate a relationship with excitement, challenges and meaning in their lives (1985). These feelings are all wonderful to have in a relationship. If, however, these ingredients are the only ones in your relationships, you are at risk for entering relationships with less than healthy males. Are you attracted to the kind of guys who are always slightly emotionally distant? No one really understands them but you, they definitely are mysterious—*challenging* is an understatement—and they have an unpredictable side. Or are you attracted to guys who are stable, predictable, nurturing and always loyal? In your head you know which type should be the best for you, but in your heart do you choose emotional excitement? Are you usually attracted to these mystery males and then you wonder why your relationships are never satisfying?

Believing that you desperately need a relationship also puts you at a high risk for relationship problems. You will usually settle for less and be attracted to people who will use you, and your fear of abandonment will not only be obvious, but will leave you open for manipulation. When we are desperate for a relationship, our self-esteem is low and we want guarantees in our lives. Ironically, at these times we are most likely to enter into relationships with the least healthy people. Eventually in these types of relationships, your intense needs will betray you. They can become overwhelming to you and at the same time overwhelm the person in your relationship. Typically, the response is for the other person to pull back. Your response is to try harder and harder. Desperately wanting a relationship and having intense needs put you at a disadvantage going into your relationship, thus increasing the probability of being used and leaving you vulnerable to problems.

High-Risk Relationships: Why Are They So Attractive?

Are you attracted to high-risk relationships? Does something about them excite you? Do you know that you should stay away from them, but you still seek them out? If so, you know the story of many adult daughters. As we have already discussed, you might find high-risk relationships attractive for a number of reasons. Let's review a few of them.

1. **High-risk relationships are exciting.**

High-risk relationships may be a lot of things, but they are not boring. Many adult daughters talk about feeling alive in these relationships and that there is always a challenge. They often state that they find reliable relationships boring, even though they want the high-risk partner to be more dependable.

2. **High-risk relationships make you feel needed.**

We all like to feel needed in a relationship. However, in most high-risk relationships the truth is that the high-risk partner needs someone to tolerate his or her behaviors. This condition is not a healthy need, but rather constitutes using people. If you don't know the difference between being needed and being used, you present a high risk for problems. Eventually, this difference occurs to most adult daughters when they begin to feel that their needs are never being met. Initially, however, the need to be needed attracts adult daughters to high-risk relationships.

3. **High-risk relationships offer freedom.**

Let's face it: A certain amount of freedom can be found in unpredictable people. Their spontaneous behaviors provide quite a ride. Many adult daughters indicate that they enter into relationships for the wrong reasons. One common reason is to flee a situation and to be free.

4. **High-risk relationships offer exclusivity.**

Exclusivity occurs when two people in a relationship have something with each other that neither of them has with anyone else. Perhaps the exclusivity comes from a knowing glance between them or a shared moment or time together that has special meaning. On the other hand, some adult daughters talk about exclusivity in their relationships by defending a high-risk partner's behavior and saying, "Oh, you don't know him like I do." Everyone else thinks his behavior is wrong, but she thinks that his actions are okay because only she knows the *real* him. This rationalization might make her feel like her relationship is exclusive, but she is also likely to feel that she must constantly defend his behavior.

The above four characteristics might apply to anyone who is attracted to high-risk relationships. However, for adult daughters another factor is at work. You might be attracted to high-risk relationships because you are a high-risk woman! In the context of relationships, a high-risk woman does not know how to take care of herself physically, emotionally or spiritually. She does not have a good understanding of what makes a healthy relationship. She is willing to take on too much responsibility for the success of a relationship. She disproportionately blames herself when things go wrong. She enters into relationships for the wrong reasons. She has observed poor relationship role models. These factors and others could place her at high risk to enter into a destructive relationship and not know how to leave it. In addition, she is likely to think that she caused all the destruction.

For example, a friend belongs to a women's support group for adult daughters. One night they allowed me to sit in and listen to the group conversations as I told them that I was going to write a book about adult daughters of alcoholics. The topic that night focused on relationships and how picking the wrong person always contributed to problems. Every member of the group talked about the pain of having picked the wrong person for a relationship at some time during their lives. When all the discussions about picking the wrong person concluded, a member of the group asked me my opinion. I replied that I wasn't sure what I thought, but listening to them did raise a question for me. My question to them was, "I have heard each of you blame yourself for picking the wrong person, and I am wondering just what makes all of you so sure that *you* picked *them?*" Maybe the people they wound up with went through relationships with multiple other women, all of whom would not tolerate their behavior. Then they all found the women in that room, all of whom have Ph.D.s in tolerance of inappropriate behavior! Before blaming the other person, adult daughters need to be sure that they are not being used because they are easy targets.

If you're in a relationship, the person is probably wrong for you if you're wondering, *If this is love, why do I feel so bad?* You have the wrong relationship partner if that person makes you feel:

- Pressured
- Confused
- Guilty about not being good enough

- Uncomfortable around him
- Scared of him
- Humiliated
- Bad about yourself
- Trapped
- Fearful about what you say

Adult Daughters' Common Relationship Problems

Besides being at high risk for relationship problems, adult daughters commonly identify five specific problems about their relationships. (Not all adult daughters, however, state that they have had all five problems.) We will discuss each of these problems in the order of how frequently they were mentioned.

Trust

When you are in a relationship, how much should you trust? What should you entrust to the other person? Do you trust yourself in your relationships? Adult daughters state that not only is the lack of trust the most common relationship problem, but also that the lack of trust takes many different forms. For example, some adult daughters do not even trust themselves to depend upon someone else for meeting any of their needs. These adult daughters believe that they must maintain an emotional distance from others at all times so that they will not be vulnerable. At the same time, adult daughters admit that their lack of self-trust makes intimacy difficult. Self-trust is related to me phobia, which we discussed earlier.

Do you trust others with the real you? Do you hide the

real you because you cannot trust that you will be accepted, or more importantly that you do not accept yourself and what you have to offer in a relationship? Lack of trust not only keeps us away from others, but it also keeps us locked within ourselves. Others cannot enter emotionally, and we cannot leave.

Other adult daughters share that they don't trust males or females at all. Still other adult daughters report the exact opposite—that they are too trusting and give their trust too easily. Have you ever found yourself more willing to trust new acquaintances rather than people you already know? If you give your trust, do you give it totally and immediately? Obviously, being either too trusting or not trusting enough puts you at a disadvantage in your relationships.

Finally, trust can be related to the problem of people-pleasing. Some adult daughters trust that pleasing the other person will lead to their own happiness. Instead, people-pleasing just leads to trying to please the other person. Your happiness is not measured by someone else's emotional state. Your happiness is a function of *your* emotional state.

Trust in a relationship begins with self, is shared with the other person, is received from the other person and is a mutual experience of the relationship. If you have trust problems in your relationship, the sharing of trust is unbalanced. An unbalanced trust situation keeps you out of balance, more concerned with the other person and less likely to have your needs met.

Intimacy

The greatest intimacy problems that adult daughters share have to do with either not allowing anyone to get close to them or not being able to become truly intimate with another person. Some adult daughters state that they experience both types of intimacy barriers in their relationships.

Do you keep people at a distance, and at the same time do you want someone with whom you can be close? Do you usually maintain a certain emotional distance in order to maintain control, not to feel vulnerable, to avoid the pain of rejection or because you fear intimacy? Many adult daughters admit that having a truly intimate relationship is one of their major desires, but at the same time they express uncertainty about allowing someone to become "too" close to them.

Several feelings underlie adult daughters' own internal mixed messages about intimacy. For example, some adult daughters talk about their fear of being intimate. These adult daughters share that their fears include fear of males, fear of the "price" of intimacy, not being able to bond with anyone, not being able to let go in their relationships and fear of rejection. Can you identify with any of these fears? If you are having difficulty with intimacy in your relationships, make a list of your fears in order to see what is holding you back.

> In my situation, my fear of abandonment holds me back. It is something in my mind. I can see my behavior over the years has built these walls in order to push him away. It's just something I am doing. So just his saying, "I'm not going anywhere," is great, but I have to solve the problem up here.
>
> *Lea Ann*

On the other hand, intimacy is a two-way street. Just because you are intimate does not automatically make your partner capable of healthy intimacy. However, as you might suspect, adult daughters who have intimacy problems in their relationships are likely to hold themselves and not their partners accountable for the problems. Remember: He can have problems that have nothing to do with you.

Kathy reports that she and her boyfriend had a big argument about a month ago and that things are better now. Recently she said that they were together and he was acting "differently." "What's wrong?" she asked, and he told her he was not feeling well. Being the good codependent, she was sure that he was not sick, but that his "illness" was really something that she had done. She kept questioning him about her behavior, refusing to accept that he was sick. Finally, he asked her why she could not accept that he was just sick and that it had nothing to do with the relationship. *You are not responsible for his problems!*

Other intimacy problems for adult daughters include having difficulty relating to their partners. Not being able to express feelings is a barrier to achieving intimacy. What do you do with your feelings in your relationships? Do you keep them to yourself, share them with your partner or share them with someone outside of your relationship? In a healthy relationship, you can share them with your partner. Most adult daughters state that they do the other two. For example, if you have a problem in your relationship, do you tell your best friend or confidante instead of your partner? Do you often fear that your partner would not understand or is not interested in your feelings? If so, you are in a relationship with intimacy problems. When this happens, do you push the other person away before he or she can disappoint you? Do you keep your partner at a distance because you feel distant from him or her?

The last type of intimacy problem occurs as a mixed message for many adult daughters who express a strong desire to be left alone, but they don't want to be lonely. When do they most want to be left alone? Usually when their feelings are most intense and typically when they are experiencing negative feelings such as sadness, upset, disappointment or hurt.

For example, when you have these feelings, is that when you are most likely to withdraw in your relationship? Ironically, if you think about it, at that time you need the most support. If you cannot let someone else in, you cannot let out your intimacy. One of the most empty feelings in the world occurs when you need other people and you want to need other people, but you do not know how to let them into your life.

Lack of achieving intimacy in your life can make you vulnerable to "love addiction," which can occur in four ways (Cowan and Kinder, 1985). You can become addicted to love out of longing, which is usually based on the lack of parental love. Wanting to be externally validated can lead to love addiction. You equate your self-worth with having your partner's approval. Therefore, you must prove your "lovability" to him. When your relationship is based on the illusion that a male is your answer to intimacy, you are at risk for love addiction. He becomes a symbol to you of your value and thus you are trapped into the illusion of finding the perfect male. Finally, love addiction occurs when you are in love with being "in love." You become a romance addict.

Self-Worth

How can my husband love me unconditionally? How can I take the emotional hook out of my gut so I can learn to grow through the bad self-talk and bad history of personal worthlessness? I need to hear over and over and over to remap my life.

Janice

Closely related to achieving intimacy in your relationships is assessing your self-worth. Self-worth can affect your relationships in many ways. Adult daughters indicate that how and what they think about themselves influences not only how they act in their relationships, but also influences the types of relationships that they have. Do you feel that you are in a relationship that accurately reflects your self-worth? For example, if you have problems in your relationship, how good do you feel about yourself? If you don't feel very good about yourself, did this occur before or after your relationship problems? When your self-worth is low, is that when you are most likely to be involved in a dysfunctional relationship? On the other hand, if your relationship begins to have problems, does your self-worth drop?

Many adult daughters "justify" their relationship problems with the feeling that they do not deserve better. Having a low self-worth puts you at a great disadvantage for trying to find a healthy relationship. Low self-worth is not always obvious. You may believe that you are very "together," but when relationship problems arise you secretly feel that you are not worthy of something better; thus, the problems are normal because of the type of person that you are. As you can see, low self-worth can lead to a self-fulfilling prophecy in a relationship. Low self-worth leads to low expectations, and when your low expectations are met, your low self-worth is reinforced.

Other ways that a low self-worth causes problems for adult daughters include never feeling good enough, not valuing yourself in your relationships, making poor choices about your partners, feeling inferior and feeling that you are unlovable. For example, do you feel different from other people and therefore expect different treatment? Does that mean that you expect to be given less than others are in your relationships? Do you frequently find yourself observing other people's "healthy" relationships and, with a deep sigh, wondering why you don't have one of those?

Another indicator of how self-worth influences your relationships is what happens to you when in the presence of your partner. Do you find yourself changing when your partner is around? We all adjust to the person in our relationship, but do you become "small" in that person's presence? Do you feel that you lose whatever identity you have left? If so, the cause is that you don't feel good about yourself. This situation can be made much worse if you are in a relationship with a very dominant or controlling male. His dominance, coupled with your low self-worth, can keep you locked into a "little-girl" relationship. He doesn't treat you as an equal and comes across more like your parent than your lover. You don't experience the respect that you should as a woman, and he easily manipulates you. One of the most destructive forms of manipulation that he can use is spouse abuse. Unfortunately, too many adult daughters share that they are trapped in abusive relationships.

The lasting effects of a low self-worth relate to why you stay in an unhealthy or destructive relationship. Quite simply, low self-worth is like a magnet that attracts you. An adult daughter might stay in a dysfunctional relationship for many different reasons. Lack of energy to leave, fear of the future, waiting for the last straw, waiting for him to change, "It's not that bad," for the sake of the children and "It's better than nothing" are all excuses of adult daughters. The reason, however, can usually be traced to a low self-worth. One of the most common statements that recovering adult daughters share is that as they become healthier, they demand healthier relationships.

Raise your self-worth and you raise your expectations in your relationships. More importantly, you begin to feel equal to your expectations. As your self-worth increases, your tolerance for inappropriate behaviors in your relationship decreases. No partner can give you your self-worth. However, a negative self-worth can be used against you and to control you. You can, though, contribute a healthy self-worth to develop and maintain a healthy relationship. Your health becomes the unspoken guideline for how the relationship will develop and grow. Self-worth is the ingredient for feeling good about yourself and your relationships. Without it, something vital and healthy is missing in your relationships—*you.*

Responsibility

Who is responsible for the success of your relationships? You, the other person or both of you? If you are a "good" adult daughter, you said that it is you. For a good relationship, both of you need to be involved. Adult daughters, though, typically feel that unless they do more than their share and assume most of the responsibilities, the relationship will fall apart. Well, what does that tell you about your style of relationships? Having too much responsibility in any relationship is bad enough, let alone having to assume the responsibility for a dysfunctional relationship. However, many adult daughters feel overly responsible for the success of a relationship.

For example, some adult daughters feel that they just can't do enough in their relationships. This feeling relates to a fear that if they didn't "do enough," things would go wrong. The feeling of responsibility is also related to control. For example, do you believe that if you assume most of the responsibility in your relationship and that you do enough, you can maintain control over the relationship? If so, you equate being responsible with being in control, which puts you in position for carrying the burdens of the relationship. Most of these burdens for adult daughters include trying to make everything okay for your partner all the time, being too loyal and living in fear of being abandoned.

I have difficulty relating to my husband. After twenty-one years of marriage, I still fear that if I make one mistake all will be lost. Intellectually, I know that this is probably unlikely, but I fear this greatly.

Angela

Other adult daughters share very different concerns about being overly responsible. These adult daughters state that they resent always having to be responsible. For example, do you ever grow tired from everyone leaning on you or all of the problems being dumped in your emotional lap? How do you feel about always having to be the strong one, the responsible one or the "I'll take care of it" one? Are you the one that everyone comes to for advice, and you'd better be right? These types of responsibilities are different from assuming that you have to do everything. Instead you are being told not only that you have to do everything, but that you are expected to do everything.

The problem is my willingness to carry the burden of the relationship and realizing much later that much more giving than receiving occurred. . . . And finally being angry that too little resulted.

Stacy

What do you believe about your expectations of responsibility in a relationship? Do you automatically expect that you will have to do more if the relationship is to be any good? Are you in a relationship with a person who is very irresponsible, thus ensuring that you must be overly responsible? On the other hand, how good are you at sharing responsibilities in your relationships? For example, are you comfortable sharing responsibilities and sharing control in your relationships? Do you secretly believe that your partner cannot do things as well as you and therefore you do it yourself?

If you are in a relationship where you are overly responsible, either by old habits or by not having a choice, you are in a relationship that is out of balance. Unfortunately, you are out of balance, too. When you overidentify with your partner by taking on the responsibilities of that person and your relationship, you underidentify with your responsibilities to yourself. In a healthy relationship, you have a "personal bill of rights." In most relationships that are out of balance, your rights are gradually eroding. For example, in the beginning you may have given your willingness to do more than your share freely and lovingly. After awhile, these responsibilities become expected of you. Finally, you feel used and taken for granted, and you begin to not only resent all of the responsibility, but also your partner. Somewhere along the progression of your relationship, you lose your rights. You lose yourself. Take your rights back. They're yours!

Picking the Wrong Person

What kind of males are you attracted to? Are you attracted to healthy males? Do you like being around them, and are you comfortable with them? Or are you attracted to males who don't appear to be healthy, but you can't resist something about them? Do you become involved with males you initially think are great, but then find yourself trying to either change or control them? Adult daughters state that they are in relationships with all of the above types of males. Unfortunately, more are involved with males who do not treat them well and meet their needs than are involved with healthy males.

Adult daughters as a group ironically rank mate selection as the fifth most common relationship problem. If you look at the first four problems, they all pertain to characteristics of adult daughters. Even though they openly share their relationship problems, adult daughters still disproportionately hold themselves accountable for the problems. As we stated before, adult daughters often look at themselves first when something goes wrong. Although engaging in self-examination is admirable, such examination can become unjustifiable self-condemnation. One would think that partners had nothing to do with creating problems in relationships! Don't excuse him for his share of the relationship problems. If you have relationship problems, don't just look in the mirror. Look across the table.

Many adult daughters state that they now recognize that they do have a choice of relationship partners. However, many are still not sure of why they make such choices. Is it something about you or something about the males that you choose, or both, that puts you at risk for picking the wrong person?

Many adult daughters share that they eagerly look forward to having a great relationship. They are aware of what an unhealthy relationship is from observing their parents. Armed with this knowledge, they believe that their relationships will be different, that they will be in loving and giving relationships, and that such relationships will be the answer to their childhood pain. Thus, many adult daughters hold the strong belief that "proper" mate selection would take them away from their emotional strife.

At the same time, many adult daughters state that they are aware of what types of males they want to avoid. Obviously, men with alcohol problems head the list. Fear of being involved with an abusive male is also very high.

> I fear getting involved with someone who has a drinking problem. In fact, when I meet guys, one of my first questions is, "Do you like to go out?" . . . hoping their response is "no" because I correlate "going out" with drinking.
>
> *Ingrid*

Males who cannot be there for them emotionally are to be avoided. We know that, regardless of good intentions, many adult daughters find themselves in relationships with the exact types of males that they want most to avoid. Regardless of the type of male—whether alcoholic, abusive or emotionally distant—these males have one thing in common: They are very controlling males.

If you have relationship problems, do you find yourself in relationships with overly controlling males? Are you constantly fighting for control in your relationships? Do you try to become more controlling in order not to be controlled? Of all the problems that adult daughters have with their relationships, being in a relationship with a controlling male is at the core of most of the problems. When you are controlled by another person, regardless of his intentional or unintentional methods, you give up your identity, your needs, your self-worth and your chance at a healthy relationship. He controls not only your relationship, but also your emotions.

If you are in a controlling relationship, how did that happen? Many adult daughters admit that they are attracted to certain males who eventually begin to control them. For example, some adult daughters are attracted to "needy" males and admit that they had looked for men whom they could rescue emotionally. At the same time, adult daughters state that these relationships in the beginning make them feel needed and useful. These types of males also need high levels of approval. Initially, this desire for approval makes her feel important to him, but the relationship dynamic soon becomes recognized for what it is: He needs to be the center of attention.

I either look for men with weaknesses that I could rescue, or I

look for men who appear strong and would let me lean on them,
only to discover they are dysfunctional.

Camille

Other adult daughters approach new relationships in just
the opposite fashion. These adult daughters share that they
are attracted to males who appear strong and in control. For
example, when they first meet, these males come across as
very open with their feelings and make statements that the
adult daughters are thinking but are too afraid to express.
Additionally, these males are usually dependable and self-
assured. Finally, they are usually decisive and can take
charge. These characteristics are initially attractive, but they
are also the same characteristics that can be used to control
others. Thus, the males are strong, but the adult daughters
do not look far enough to see if the males are also
dysfunctional.

Many adult daughters state that, once relationship problems emerge, they find either working through the problems
or breaking free from them quite difficult. The divorce rate
for adult daughters is 12 percent higher than for women from
nonalcoholic homes. Therefore, many adult daughters can
end bad relationships, but the statistic also tells us that many
adult daughters are not able to resolve relationship problems.

Another problem arises for many adult daughters when
they try either to totally control their relationships or, if they
are being controlled, try to become countercontrolling.
These adult daughters are in relationships with males who
give up total control to them. Again, initially this situation
appears attractive. However, soon the adult daughters deteriorate into feeling that they are taking care of a "little boy"
and that they are being asked to play more the role of a
mother than a lover or spouse. Resentment soon dominates
these relationships.

Countercontrolling develops in a relationship as a response to being overly controlled and trying to fight back. Adult daughters who experience these types of relationships share that they are constantly fighting with or having to manipulate their partners in order to not only control their dysfunctional behaviors, but also in order to reduce their control. Unfortunately, either way these adult daughters are in a controlling relationship characterized by a constant power struggle.

Finally, some adult daughters are in healthy relationships. Some of these adult daughters are aware of the quality of their relationships and enjoy them fully. Other adult daughters in healthy relationships admit that they have difficulty enjoying them, usually because of a fear that the relationship would not last, or a constant fear about whether they are doing the right things in the relationship. Their fears are that they would drive away the other person.

Whatever your current relationship, being controlled, living with an alcoholic or living with some other type of dysfunctional person is not what you deserve. You have a right to relationship happiness. However, no matter how hard you try, you cannot be responsible for your partner's happiness. You can support it, encourage it and share it, but you cannot *be* it. You cannot do everything for the other person and thus make them happy. You can, however, lose yourself in the process of trying and lose your own happiness as a result.

Do adult daughters have healthy relationships? Yes. Can you have a healthy relationship? Yes. Think about the fact that one of the largest groups of people who are acutely aware of the power of healthy relationships and have a desire to be in them are adult daughters of alcoholics. Use your knowledge to lead you to what you want. This chapter opened by asking you what you expect from your relationships and what your definition is of a healthy relationship. Raise your expectations. Find out what is healthy. Become the healthiest person you can be. Refuse to tolerate unhealthy behaviors in your relationships, and you will begin to establish the ingredients necessary for successful, healthy relationships. Unhealthy and controlling males are trouble with a capital T. They will offer their controlling invitations to you and hope that you will accept. Tell them that you are too healthy to attend!

Avoid relationships that appear to have great potential "if only he'll change." In that type of relationship, you're assuming that you can change him. He will continue to do what he does, but probably even more once you are in the relationship. Remember that he usually is on his good behavior when you first start dating. Stay clear of the "he'll change" project. If you remove the apostrophe from "he'll," you'll see what you have left. The only one who will change is you, and you will not like what you will become. As a matter of fact, you may end up with the exact opposite of what you wanted your life to be. Becoming involved with a high-risk male is the first step of the last thing that you want to do. Meeting someone who is right for you is easier than creating him.

The power of a relationship can never be underestimated. The relationship that you had with your parents while growing up is still with you. The hopes that a new relationship brings are tremendous. The love and beauty of a healthy relationship can add to your life beyond measure, but the devastation of a dysfunctional relationship may never end. Your quest for a healthy relationship and being in a positive relationship must always come in addition to your health and not be a substitute for it. A healthy you is the first step to healthier relationships. Take care of yourself, and have a positive relationship with yourself. You deserve it!

For me, love. I did not love myself, therefore I could not genuinely love someone else. Today I love myself a little and, boy, am I reaching out! I can't wait until I love myself a lot. This may take one minute, one hour, one day or one year. That is not important, for I know it will come!

Rhonda

Keeper Hole

You can recirculate for a long time
In relationships that feel like your childhood.
You think you're trying to get out
But all the forces from your past
Conspire to kick you back in.

Pretty soon you're so busy trying to stay alive
That you forget how you got there,
Or why you stay there,
Or whether you want to be there.
But you know it's an old, familiar pain.

And you keep going back in,
Thinking that if you could just get
That elusive something your soul craves,
Just this one time, it would heal all your past,
All your pain, all your problems.

Or you fight it. Thinking that if only
You could win this familiar battle,
You'd finally defeat the ancient foe;
The triumphant, final "NO!" hurled
At someone who no longer exists.

The only way out is to become whole.

Alison Snow Jones

AFTERTHOUGHTS

The easiest kind of relationship for me
is with ten thousand people. The hardest is with one.

JOAN BAEZ

People change and forget to tell each other.

LILLIAN HELLMAN

I have an inalienable, constitutional and natural right
to love whom I may, to love as long or as short a period
as I can, to change that love every day I please!

VICTORIA WOODHULL

I seem to have an awful lot of people inside me.

EDITH EVANS

It is hard to fight an enemy who has outposts in your head.

SALLY KEMPTON

Chapter 13

Perfect Parenting

What I have found myself doing is all the things I swore I would never do to my children and not knowing any other alternatives. This is especially true when I'm under a great deal of stress, which doesn't really have anything to do with my children.

Jessica

Next to relationships, problems about parenting are the second most important concern for adult daughters. Whether or not they have children, adult daughters express strong opinions and emotions about their parenting skills. Their concerns range from not wanting children to wanting to be the perfect parent. Adult daughters who do not want children say they are afraid to have children because of emotional burnout from their own childhoods—that is, lack of energy (or exhaustion) from having to parent themselves or their siblings (or both) while growing up in an alcoholic household.

Other adult daughters want children very much or already have children. Their concerns reflect their desires to be the best parents they can, wanting their children to have "normal" childhoods and a fear that they cannot accomplish these things successfully. Whether they want children or not, the common bond among adult daughters about parenting is fear.

If you are a parent or think you will become one, what are your expectations and fears about parenting? Do you believe that you have the necessary skills to be a healthy parent? Do you want to raise your children differently from how you were raised? Have you found yourself saying that you will never do to your children what was done to you? Are you afraid, however, that you might repeat the same family patterns of your childhood? If so, all these emotions are normal for adult daughters.

Adult daughters can be healthy parents in spite of these fears. Many healthy mothers are adult daughters. Adult daughters, however, remain acutely aware of not only their own childhoods, but also the influences from childhood that might be carried into their own parenting careers. These concerns led adult daughters to talk openly about their feelings and anxieties regarding parenting.

Does this discussion raise any concern you might have about your parenting skills? Nothing can put you in touch with your own childhood memories faster than being in charge of your children's childhoods. Maybe you don't remember much about elementary school, but when your child starts school, the memories will come flooding back.

For example, do you remember crayons and coloring in first grade? When you smell a crayon today, does it remind you of many years ago? More importantly, as you begin to parent and your child begins to respond emotionally, you will begin to feel again many of your own childhood emotions. Your ability to work through your own childhood issues and separate them successfully from your parenting skills will become quite important.

Your ability to parent successfully is related to your ability to give beyond yourself. We discussed this earlier when we talked about generativity. We have talked consistently throughout this book about adult daughters giving so much of themselves to others. At times adult daughters seem to be saying that giving of themselves is what they do best. When your talent for giving beyond yourself will be most needed, is that the time you'll express your greatest doubts about being able to do so successfully? All parents doubt their abilities. Adult daughters are very open about their doubts, but some also share concerns that are definitely related to being an adult daughter as well as being a parent.

I fear being like my mom. I fear destroying my child's self-esteem. I fear being too controlling, overprotective, then over-compensating and having no control. I fear my children hating me. I have no trust in my own judgment. . . . I expect perfection from myself and my kids.

Cindy

Do you know what your parenting concerns are? Are you overly aware of trying to ensure that your children have a normal childhood? Do you try to do too much to make their upbringing normal, thus unknowingly making it different for them anyway? Do you want your children to be able to express themselves and be free to try new behaviors, but at the same time expect them to be compliant?

Are you silently saying, *I want my children to have a different childhood than I did, but I expect them to behave the same as I do?* This feeling is not unusual for adult daughters. Research indicates that adult daughters who are parents have a higher expectation of compliant behavior in children than do women raised in nonalcoholic families who are now parents. This mixed message is delivered to your children: Be different, but be like me!

I'm quick to use guilt and emotion, subtly used on me, to get desired results from my children.

Lucille

Why do adult daughters expect so much obedience from their children? Usually because as children themselves they were compliant for fear of rocking the boat. As daughters of alcoholics, they learned quickly to read other people and to be overly sensitive. Don't worry if your children are not like you. After all, you may take that as an indicator that you are doing a good job. In families not under stress, children don't have to be emotionally on guard and can do what they do best—be children.

Adult daughters express many concerns about their parenting abilities. We will discuss the four most common, in order of how frequently they were mentioned. If you identify with these issues, you are probably a normal adult daughter who is expressing her normal parenting concerns. Now the challenge is to see if you can be a normal parent! (Don't worry, you don't have to be normal perfectly.)

1. **Control**

Not this again. It's everywhere. Control, control, control! Can't we get away from this? Many adult daughters share that their control issues interfere with their parenting skills. Do you have any control problems with your parenting? Do you know what they are?

> My own perfectionism and problems with the "child" part of me have caused my parenting problems. I find myself having difficulty having fun. . . . I find myself holding him back and not enjoying him as fully as I might. I have to consciously hold myself back and allow him freedom to be.
>
> *Susie*

Control problems affect parenting skills for adult daughters in several different ways. For example, many adult daughters admit they want too much control over their children, but are afraid to let go. They exercise their controlling behaviors by taking on too many of the responsibilities for the children. Other adult-daughter mothers express that they find it difficult to allow their children to be free. They overly protect them, resulting in the adult daughter not being able to find a balance between "mothering" and "smothering" her children. Your overly developed need to control can impede their normal abilities to develop. Are you overly controlling? Ask yourself, do you allow your family to work out its problems or do you "take charge"?

> I struggle with needing to overprotect for fear of losing yet another precious part of me.
>
> *Courtney*

Control problems become evident when you believe you must be the "perfect parent." This role is obviously a continuation of the one many adult daughters know well and have never abandoned. An indicator of this problem is taking your parental role too seriously. You learn to take care of your children quantitatively, but not qualitatively. Children need laughter, easy times, fun and many different ways of expressing emotions. Taking yourself too seriously not only takes these options away from your children, but it also keeps them away from you.

Are you afraid you will damage your child if you make a mistake? Do you have a hard time telling your child "no" because you fear losing her love? Do you feel inadequate as a parent if you can't give everything? Are you afraid your child will not love you if you show anger to her or she becomes angry with you? Do you find it difficult to accept that your children are less than perfect? Do you have incredibly high expectations for your children? Have your children, when upset, told you that they cannot be "perfect like you"? If so, you possess some of the indicators of needing a lot of control over your children. These indicators all show that you are still having control problems as an adult daughter.

If you do have control problems, begin to work on them. Don't go overboard. Remember that your children need many of your positive skills as an adult daughter in order to grow. They need your guidance, empathy, compassion and survival skills. They also need your love and support, and they need their own emotional arena to use them. If you want your children's childhood to be different from your own, and you are having parenting problems, you may have to become different. The healthiest thing for a child is a healthy parent, not a controlling one.

2. **I don't know how to parent**

Do you ever question your parenting skills because you are not sure of what you are doing? If so, not only are you like all parents, but adult daughters ask this question even more than other parents. Many adult daughters express that they just don't trust their own abilities to parent. This fear usually relates to the role modeling they observed but that left them without many ideas about how to parent successfully. This lack of self-assurance contributes to their fears that they might hurt their children by repeating many of the family patterns they most wanted to avoid, the ones that hurt them when they were young.

If you find yourself fearing that you do not know how to parent, what are your options? One option is to do what you know, which—given what they know—is not what most adult daughters want to do. The other is to seek information about parenting. Involve yourself in parenting groups that teach healthy skills. Share your emotional concerns by joining parent support groups or Adult Children of Alcoholics groups.

Many places are available where you can learn positive parenting techniques. Your local schools, colleges and community mental-health centers often offer courses in parenting. Don't be afraid to go for help. Remember that you want your children to trust you, and they want to trust that you know what you are doing.

Being uncertain about parenting skills often leads to uncertainty about normal behavior in children. If you use your own childhood as the encyclopedia of childhood behaviors, your knowledge of how "normal" children act would be quite limited. One of the most common problems for many adults who have problems parenting is a low level of knowledge about normal human development. Again, seek out resources in your community to increase your level of knowledge about children and their normal behaviors.

> I had to go to a parenting class and find healthy role models.
>
> *Claire*

Gaining knowledge about normal human development becomes easier to accomplish when you have a realistic perception of what normal is. Additionally, learning about parenting and child development can help you overcome your perceptions that you need to be the perfect parent who is raising the perfect child. You should find relief in discovering that all parents make mistakes, children don't always do what they should and yet healthy families still develop.

Besides, perfectionism is not all that it is supposed to be. After all, when you're perfect, you have no place to go and few people to whom you can turn. If you want your children to be healthy and to turn to you, let them know that you are human. Believing that you must be the perfect parent will always leave you doubting, make you lonely and make it difficult for your children to feel close to you. No one, including you, can ever live up to expectations of perfection.

3. **Lack of consistency**

How consistent are you as a parent? Is the atmosphere in your house consistent, or does it shift unpredictably? Are you stable in your feelings toward your children, or do you have "parental mood swings"? Many adult daughters talk about consistency problems in parenting. After all, how consistent was your house when you were growing up? Did the situation change instantly if one of your parents came home drinking? Did the mood of your family shift to reflect the unpredictable moods of your parents?

Parental inconsistency for adult daughters falls into two categories: mood (or feeling) inconsistencies and behavior inconsistencies.

For example, some adult daughters share that they cannot control their mood swings, causing them to be too loving sometimes and too distant at other times. Other adult daughters indicate that they had a hard time staying in their parenting role.

> My daughter has parented me most of her seventeen years.
>
> *Sheila*

Some adult daughters state that they can be physically available for their children, but they are not always emotionally present. Many adult daughters question their abilities to be fair with their children. Although all parents would like more patience, adult-daughter parents openly express that they often vacillate in how much patience they have, which leads many of them to question whether they are consistent with their feelings with their children.

On the other hand, many adult-daughter parents expect their children to be consistent in *their* behaviors and moods. Many adult daughters state that allowing *their* children to express different moods is difficult, because their children should always be content. Even when the children of adult daughters voice normal anger or anxiety, disproportionate anxiety frequently arises in the adult daughter because of her desire to want to control everything. Someone else's anxiety can make you uncomfortable if you think the anxiety is your fault or that you should do something about it.

Finally, inconsistency fears are related to adult daughters' difficulty in accepting differences between their children and themselves in behaviors, feelings and attitudes. When you think your children should be like you, and they are not, your expectations are not met. Some adult daughters are afraid that if they show their disapproval for different behaviors, they could inhibit normal autonomy in their children. Others talk about how inconsistency interferes with their bonding with their children.

4. **Not being able to meet your child's needs**

My lost childhood and I do not have the energy or a heart big enough to really be the parent I feel a child should have.

Ellen

Do you ever fear that you cannot adequately nurture your child? Are you afraid that you cannot meet your child's emotional needs? Do you ever wonder if you are ignoring your child's needs? Do you feel you cannot provide for your child's needs because yours were not met? If so, you share some common concerns with other adult-daughter parents.

Adult daughters express in several different ways their fears about not being able to meet a child's needs. Some adult daughters are concerned that they cannot love unconditionally. Others are not sure they can express openly their approval to their children.

Some adult daughters believe they can meet their child's needs if they just protect the child from unpleasantness. Wanting the child to meet the adult daughter's needs is not an uncommon feeling. The desire to have someone love us, need us and rely on us is strong. On the other hand, we must remember to reciprocate. Related to this problem is when you see your children as a second chance for your own childhood. Unfortunately, trying to relive your childhood through theirs will not help your children. You can have a healthier parenthood by enjoying your child.

Sometimes the key to healthy parenting is to make sure we grow up before our children do. You will find that as you meet your children's needs, your needs as a parent will start to be met. Not everything will be smooth, but you can achieve a balance of needs in your relationship with your children, even though the exchange won't be 50-50. Your children need a lot from you. A balanced exchange is when you give as much as you can and still maintain your emotional health. At the same time, your children can make you feel glad to be a parent every now and then.

Remember, you are allowed to meet your needs as well. We become out of balance as parents when we forget that. When you are trying to have your own needs met, remember that you have adult needs and children cannot meet all adult needs. Your needs as an adult must be met by other adults and you.

Did you identify with the above concerns of adult-daughter parents? I am sure you can add to the list of problems, fears and emotions.

A situation that puts additional pressure on adult daughters is the social pressure to become "superwoman." The media image that you must do absolutely everything for your children, your relationships, your profession, your body and your mind and do it all with a smile on your face will leave you totally burned out.

In order to have a "good day" you need forty-two hours (*USA Today*, 1989)! We're even supposed to set aside time each day for "meaningful interaction" with our plants! Information and pressure like this will make you not only exhausted, but also disappointed in yourself because you cannot be and do all things. Superwomen aren't supposed to have good days; they are supposed to have "perfect days." Such expectations, though, only leave you feeling as if you don't have enough time in your day. You'll feel that you can never do enough. If you allow yourself to succumb to the pressure of "superwomen," you will feel that your only solution is to try even harder, and you will become burned out quickly on parenting. Parenting is for life, but parenting is not (for the most part) a life sentence. Conserve your energy and use it wisely. Do not let the superwoman image consume you. When your parenting energy becomes consumed, it must be replaced. You cannot replace it by becoming a better parent, but you can replace it by taking better care of yourself, which will help make you a better parent.

As adult children, we are extremely aware of the influence that family has on children. We are extremely aware of how important healthy relationships are between parents and between parents and their children. However, we must be aware that we are at risk for extreme self-criticism and self-doubt about our parenting skills. To say that we want to do a good job is fine, but at the same time we are not sure of what we want to do. We tell our children to try alternatives, express their feelings, act their ages and have fun. If this advice is so good for our children, maybe we should try it ourselves. Don't let your unresolved childhood issues or fear of parenting skills hold you back.

You are probably a much better parent than you think. You may have behaviors that put you at risk, but you also have some of the greatest assets to be a healthy parent. You have a desire to want to do a good job. You have the ability to recognize needs in others. You are not afraid to become involved. You know the power of parents.

Do you want to be a healthy parent? If so, work through your doubts, find resolution to your own childhood issues, learn appropriate parenting skills and use those parts of you that are healthy. All children need guidance, love, support, nurturing and acceptance. So do parents.

> The most important thing about my relationship with my daughter is that I allow her to be herself and I appreciate her for what she is. As I watch her grow, the most valuable part of my parenting is having her appreciate who she is, having her love herself . . . having her feel she has a right to be here and to ask for what she needs to be happy. It's okay to be just the way she is. . . . It's okay to be angry and it's okay to do the wrong things and that Mama's going to love you anyway. No matter what you do. And she does have that attitude about herself.
>
> *Evelyn*

AFTERTHOUGHTS

What is buried in the past of one generation
falls to the next to claim.

SUSAN GRIFFIN

We thought we were running away from the grownups,
and now we are the grownups.

MARGARET ATWOOD

The doctors told me I would never walk, but my mother
told me I would, so I believed my mother.

WILMA RUDOLPH

If you can't make a mistake, you can't make anything.

MARVA N. COLLINS

My father turned my life around by insisting
I be more than I was and by believing I could be more.

OPRAH WINFREY

Part Five

Discovery and Recovery

Chapter 14

I Think I Can, I Think I Can

Remember the story, *The Little Engine That Could*? The little engine was asked to pull all of the train cars over the mountain because the big engine broke down. "I can't do it because I'm too small," stated the little engine, and it did not want to help. The other cars, however, told the little engine that if it did not help they would not be able to make it over the mountain. At this point, the story becomes a codependent tale. All of a sudden, the responsibility for the big cars is placed on the little engine. What does the little engine do? It allows itself to get talked into trying and codependently begins to pull the other cars up the mountain. The little engine spends the entire time pulling and telling itself, *I think I can, I think I can*. The little engine is not sure it can do it, but because the effort is for someone else, the engine is willing to expend all of its energy trying. Eventually, the little engine makes it to the other side of the mountain and discovers its own great strength.

Are there any similarities between this story and you? Can you make it to the other side of Recovery Mountain? Do you realize that you have been pulling the weight of others for so long and that you have great strength? Do you realize that even though you may have been doing things codependently, you are capable of making transitions in your life to meet your own needs? Have you discovered your strengths, capabilities and spirit, which you can now use for yourself? Have you ever thought *I think I can, I think I can* about your own potential for recovery?

Throughout this book you have been on a journey of discovery and recovery. What have you discovered about yourself? Do you have a better understanding of who you are and what you want in your life? Do you want to change? Will you change? Will you buy a ticket on the recovery train or will you sell it to others? As an adult daughter, you have something today that you did not have in childhood: *You have a choice!* You can stay where you are. You can keep those things that you learned painfully that serve you well today. You can work through and learn to let go of your grief and losses. You can build upon your strength. You do have choices. Will you use them?

No one can tell you what to choose or what to change. You are the explorer who is discovering herself. On your journey you are identifying those places that you do not want to visit again. You are also finding those places in you that are warm, confident and full of hope that you will want to visit over and over again in order to find more energy to go even farther on your journey. Will I tell you how to travel? No, but I will share the map that many recovering adult daughters have shared with me.

Desire for Change

Do you have a desire to change your life, your attitudes and your feelings? Would you like to be free of the emotional baggage that you carry as an adult daughter? Do you find yourself wondering why you cannot enjoy life as much as you would like, but you admit that you would like to try? If so, you are not alone. In addition to all of the issues that we have discussed so far in this book, the desire for change is equally strong among adult daughters. As perceptive, intuitive and empathic as they are about others, adult daughters are equally energetic about their own behaviors and feelings, once they are discovered. However, adult daughters are more likely to use their emotional skills on others than on themselves.

Can you convert your desire for change into action? Many adult daughters did and their insights appear throughout this chapter. Recovering adult daughters share five common themes of advice for other adult daughters who would like to recover: Use your past, take care of yourself, recognize what you have missed, join a recovery group and find healthy people to be around.

Use Your Past

Do you realize that your past can be a tool for recovery? You can convert your survival skills into growing skills. Don't be afraid of your past, and don't allow it to become "eternal." Do you believe that because you once were affected negatively, you will always be affected negatively? The only thing that can make a negative past worse is to allow it to affect the rest of today. Because you are an adult daughter, do you have to die one more day because of it? Are you through giving up your days to the past?

Your traumatic childhood is over. Yes, the pain can still be there, but you can use your strength to break its hold on you. You were victimized by alcohol; don't be victimized by your past. We must remember to keep the label of ACOA in perspective. "ACOA" tells us where we have been, yet it need not predict where we are going. If we give the label that predictive power, we are codependent on the label.

Read, learn and grow, but don't use the ACOA label as an excuse for being dysfunctional. Don't become immersed in ACOA issues to the point where it becomes a dysfunction itself.
Stella

Take Care of Yourself

How many times have you told yourself, *I better take care of (fill in the blank)?* Until now, someone else's name has always appeared in that space. Recovering adult daughters are telling you to put yourself first. They are telling you to take care of yourself. You do not have to be a caretaker. You are not in charge of the universe. However, you are in charge of yourself. What do you do for yourself? Can you make a list of how you take care of yourself? Could you convince someone who is concerned about you that you are taking good care of yourself?

> You can care without being a caretaker for everyone. You have to put yourself first and not last. To be self-caring is not selfish.
>
> *Glenna*

Be kinder to yourself. Learn to let go of the unrealistic expectations that you place on yourself. You have a right to your own needs, and using your rights is the first step toward taking care of yourself. The best statement that I know for adult daughters appears in the *Desiderata*, and it simply and eloquently states, "You have a right to be here."

Taking care of yourself means that you are taking responsibility for your own growth. Do not fear your growth. Do not put off growing because you fear that working through your feelings will be painful. Remember, growing pains are less severe and healthier than past pains. Give yourself time to change. True change is measured in small steps, in what you do daily.

As you begin to take care of yourself, watch out for depression. Feeling the emotions of working through your past is normal, as is finding yourself becoming angry over issues that you have denied for a long time. When you start to feel overwhelmed by what you have discovered about yourself or by your journey of recovery, slow down. No one said that you had to recover perfectly. No one said that you must forgive every transgression in your life. The journey is yours; you're the engineer. If you start to feel depressed, find a rest stop.

Taking care of yourself means putting your needs first. This behavior is unusual for many adult daughters. Take your time. Taking care of yourself will be easier when you feel better about yourself. Take the time to do things that make you feel good about yourself. You will find that you are simultaneously beginning to take care of yourself.

Recognize What You Have Missed

Discovery is not only recognizing how you were victimized, but also realizing what you have missed. Are you aware of what you have missed? More importantly, are you willing to try to retrieve it now? The greatest pain from the past continues when it keeps us from recovering what we missed.

My hope for the future is just to have peace. One of the big secrets of my program is not to look ahead . . . to try, except for necessary planning, not to even look to the next hour, but to savor the moment. That's not something I've ever done in my entire life. I lived my whole life planning and building walls and avoiding disasters that were inevitable. Now I've learned to just savor the moment, to accept whatever life is offering me now. It's not that I don't have hope; it's just that I have faith that when tomorrow comes, whatever it is, it's going to be right for me. That allows me to enjoy today.

Harriet

When you become aware of what you want because you know something is missing in your life, you begin to find a purpose and a direction for your recovery. Retrieving what you have missed can be a goal. Becoming the kind of person that you would like to be gives you direction. If you are not sure of what you want to do, don't spend all of your energy trying to figure it out before you begin your recovery. You can start right now by asking yourself what you *don't* want to do. Many times knowing what we don't want can lead us into the right direction by keeping us away from the things we don't desire. For example, if you don't want to stay as you are, you don't want to be isolated, you don't want to keep the family secret to yourself, you don't want to keep having relationship problems and you don't want to keep all the pain inside anymore, you have found out a lot about yourself. You can use this self-discovery to begin your journey just as much as you can use your knowledge of how you would like to change. The important thing is to start your journey, not decide on your destination. Don't add missing the journey to your list of what is missing in your life. All you have to know is that when you say, "Do I know what is missing in my life?" your answer can be, "Recovery, and I'm going to find it."

Join a Recovery Group

We did the best we could, but we did it alone—no more.

Ginny

You don't have to recover alone. As a matter of fact, you will recover faster and better with the help of other people. One of the best ways to overcome feelings of uniqueness and isolation is to be with other people. Find a good support group and get involved. Many options are available to you. You can go to Al-Anon meetings for adult children. You can find independent ACOA groups. You can try women's support groups. You can become involved in counseling or therapy groups. The important thing is that you are involved.

You will be better able to confront your feelings when people who understand not only you, but also the dynamics of alcoholic families, surround you. Don't be afraid to ask a counselor what she or he knows about adult children issues. If the counselor is not comfortable with or knowledgeable about adult children, find someone who is. Remember, you are the consumer of your recovery. Ask for what you need.

> What I'm hoping to accomplish from being in this group is to find out who I am and what I like to do. I know some things, but a lot of the things that I think and believe seem to be things I picked up from my dad. . . . I don't really know if that's me. So I am trying to understand me and I am still discovering.
>
> *Nan*

If you try a group and your needs are not being met, don't give up on the idea of growth through groups. Try another group. In fact, you might try at least six different groups before you think about giving up. Groups and counselors are still learning how to meet the needs of adult children, and mistakes are made. Some adult groups are not as healthy as others. After all, no one said that adult support groups have to be perfect. As a matter of fact, maybe the ones who are trying to be perfect are the least healthy. If your group reminds you of your alcoholic family, find another group.

Also, remember that you will not find in an adult children's group everything you are looking for in your recovery. Your adult children's group can provide emotional support, but you can attend other groups to learn about skills and knowledge that you are missing. For example, you can learn relationship and communication skills, self-esteem techniques, assertiveness training and parenting skills in a variety of other types of support groups and training workshops.

Remember, you don't have to alcoholize all of your recovery. You are much more than an adult daughter, and you have a diversity of talents and needs. Growth is for all the parts of you, even though in many cases the "adult daughter" part has held you back. Go and do it all. Become the healthiest *you*, not the healthiest adult daughter!

Find Healthy People

As you discover yourself, you will discover that you have less tolerance for unhealthy behaviors. The healthier you become, the more aware you become of unhealthy people. One of the best ways to learn healthy behavior is to be around healthy people, which will become more important to you as you begin to change. For example, those people who know you the best as an adult daughter are often the ones who will be the most resistant to the new you. These people share a common history with you, they have relied on you to meet their needs, and they need you to be in your supporting role. Now you are taking the lead role, and they are not sure how to react. What will they do? Usually they will do what they do best: respond to you in their old ways. Will you fall back into your old habits, or will the recovering you step forward?

For example, one of the best indicators of discovery and recovery is the desire to share what you have learned. Where do many adult daughters want to share their growth? Unfortunately, some adult daughters want to share their growth where the problems began. Wrong move! Say that you visit your family of origin and they are playing the same old dysfunctional song. What do you do? Do you sing along, since you know the words by heart? Or do you learn to respond to them differently? They will always try to pull you back, because the old you is the person that they know best. The old you meets their needs. They will try to push your buttons, which is not unusual given that your family installed them!

Separating yourself from unhealthy behaviors will be easier when you have healthy friends and relationships to go to.

Your responsibility is not to make your family healthy. Don't fall into the role of family counselor. Be on guard for this trap. Once you start to grow and deal with the alcoholism in your life, you become the new family expert. They will try to use you by pulling you back and trying to manipulate you with all of the old emotional buttons. If you no longer want to sing the dysfunctional song, find healthy people and you'll have new music in your life.

Discovery and recovery take time. You will pass through different stages on your journey of growth. Each stage will have its benefits, as well as traps that can keep you from going farther. For example, don't confuse recovery with something else. Don't confuse it with self-discovery or awareness. When you first discover that many of your behaviors are normal for an adult daughter, you'll likely experience a sense of relief. You'll feel better about yourself. This step is a discovery step, not a recovery step. Don't confuse relief for recovery. When you are injured and the pain stops, you feel relief, but relief does not mean healing.

Each stage of discovery brings relief. Enjoy it. Use it to gather energy for the next stage and then go on. You deserve recovery. Don't settle for anything less. You have the right to ask for everything. Above all, as you go through the different stages, be aware of the "awareness trap." You might become so preoccupied with wanting to recover perfectly and learning all of the proper steps that you lose sight of your reasons for recovery. You become so trapped into memorizing and learning the process that you forget the end results. The idea of recovery is to get there, not memorize the road that is taking you there.

As you attempt to change you will probably go through several stages.

Recognition

The first stage of recovery is recognizing the presence of the movement of recovery from alcoholism. This movement has expanded so much in the last several years that millions of people are experiencing it for the first time. The movement is one of both recovery and community. You will recognize the community; more importantly, you will recognize in yourself that you want to recover and become part of this community.

You will recognize that how you were influenced and how you are living is not what you want. You will recognize that alternatives are available and that you want to try them. You will recognize the most important part of recovery: yourself.

Involvement

Involvement in recovery can occur in two ways: intellectually and emotionally. Most adult daughters share that they have no problems becoming involved intellectually with recovery. For example, they want to learn everything about adult children, alcoholism, dysfunctional families and troubled relationships. They are willing to read all of the books, attend all of the ACOA conferences they can find and discuss the issues for hours. As adult children, if we could recover by doing it intellectually, we would have the healthiest minds in the world!

Most adult daughters are not afraid to say what they think. Many have problems, however, identifying their emotions and expressing them. Involvement in your recovery requires emotional involvement. You cannot recover by what you know. You recover by *feeling* what you know. If you are afraid of your feelings, you will fear involvement. Adult daughters are open about the emotional barrier that keeps them from becoming involved in recovery. Rationalizing, minimizing and intellectually justifying our pain can be easier than feeling it and working through it. Don't confuse knowledge with emotions. Otherwise, you will "know" recovery, but never "feel" it.

Wanting to Change

As you become more aware of yourself and your alternatives, you can become more aware of wanting to change. However, make sure you are aware of the direction in which you would like to change. Don't become caught in the cycle of wanting to change everything about you. After all, you have many admirable qualities that brought you this far. Don't throw the best parts of you away because you think that you must change.

Additionally, change takes time. You have been an adult daughter for a long time, and you were the child of an alcoholic long before that. Give yourself time to change. You don't have to do it all at once, nor do you have to do it completely. You set the pace. If you put too many expectations on yourself in too short a time, you will be doing the exact same thing that everyone else did to you for so long.

> Have patience. . . . You must give it time. We didn't get sick overnight, and we're not going to get better overnight. Nurture your strengths. You are a survivor. . . . Be very patient and gentle with yourself. . . . Go slow, determine what works for you. Take it easy and don't rush.
>
> *Tess*

Finding Help

When you first find help you will validate your awareness. You will find a lot of comfort when you realize that others share many of your feelings and ideas. However, many adult daughters reach the "discovery plateau" at this point and don't know how to go any farther. They join support groups and discuss their lives, feelings, doubts, needs and emotions, but they are not able to transform into action their insights or the support that they receive. Many adult children who go into support groups stay at the same level of awareness about their problems and are unable to find a way to change their lives (Ackerman, 1989).

When you find help, make sure that you also find a way to convert the support that you are receiving into ways for you to recover. Knowledge without a way to use it creates frustration. You have lived enough frustration in your life by not being able to change others. You can, however, avoid developing frustrations about yourself by turning your knowledge into action.

Living Your Recovery

To feel the spirituality in me is the peace and joy that I wake up with in the morning and that I carry with me throughout the day—the joy in my heart to be alive. That's a real blessing for me. I'm grateful to be alive and I never was before. That's my sense of spirituality. To know God is with me and forgives me, even before I am able to forgive myself.

Anne

Recovery is for living, not discussing. The last stage of recovery is applying what you have learned. Again, you do not have to recover all at once. Many adult daughters realize that the exact traits that characterize adult daughters are the worst ones to have when it comes to recovery. Perfectionism, denial, control, overresponsibility, lack of trust and low self-esteem are not good building blocks for recovery. As a matter of fact, these characteristics can be your worst enemies.

An important part of undertaking recovery is recognizing "recovery lag" (Ackerman, 1987): Not all parts of the adult daughter are affected negatively, not all parts need the same amount of intervention, and not all parts recover at the same rate. Some parts of your recovery will take longer than others. Some phases of your recovery will leap ahead, and some phases will lag behind. After all, some of your issues are more emotional and more painful than others, and they will need more time. Recovery is not a contest. You don't have to do recovery perfectly, and you don't have to do it better than everyone else.

Finally, recovery is for *you*. Many adult daughters feel that recovery would be better and easier for someone else. Maybe it would. The problem is that the adult daughter will never know. You cannot recover for another person and no one can recover for you, not that it hasn't been tried. A lot of codependent traps are in place along the way to recovery. Keep the focus on you, and you can avoid them.

What is the goal of recovery? You are. The object of recovery is not only to find you, but also to be yourself. Use whatever you can to find recovery. Use the strengths that you have developed, even if they were codependent, to pull yourself up and over your own mountain. Find the other side of your mountain. Find the other side of you. Don't stop because you feel small. Don't let the journey overwhelm you, and don't worry about where it will lead. The important thing is to begin. What is the best time to start your journey? Now. Don't wait for someone else's permission. Tell them to keep their codependency to themselves. You have an important place to go. You have your ticket, your emotional baggage, your strength and your map. Now go! Find *your* recovery!

> *If I am not for myself, who will be for me?*
> *If I am not for others, who am I for?*
> *And if not now, when?*
>
> The Talmud

AFTERTHOUGHTS

When we were children, we used to think that when we were grown-up we would no longer be vulnerable. But to grow up is to be accepting vulnerability. . . . To be alive is to be vulnerable.

MADELEINE L'ENGLE

When we can't dream any longer, we die.

EMMA GOLDMAN

*If only we'd stop trying to be happy,
we'd have a pretty good time.*

EDITH WHARTON

*Don't wait around for other people to be happy for you.
Any happiness you get you've got to make yourself.*

ALICE WALKER

*Being defeated is often a temporary condition.
Giving up is what makes it permanent.*

MARILYN VOS SAVANT

Chapter 15

To Self, with Love, from Daughter

Can you make the transition from being an adult daughter
of an alcoholic to being your own person? Can you make the
transition from codependence to independence? Can you
leave the shadow of the past to find your place in the sun? Is
your identity dependent upon where you have been, or is it
developing and changing to meet where you are going? You
can do all of these things. You can become your own person,
overcome codependent behaviors and find balance in your
life. However, how will you know when you have become
your own person? How will you know that your past no
longer dominates you and that you are becoming a healthy
adult?

Your answers will depend upon not only your perceptions
of recovery, but also upon your ability to live your recovery.
For example, if someone accused you of recovering, could
they find enough evidence to convict you? We know that
you intellectually understand the issues of adult daughters.
We know that you can change if you want. We know that
you have choices. We don't know, however, whether you
will change enough to become your own person.

Becoming your own person will require using all of your
adult-daughter skills to care for a new, special person in your
life. You will need to transfer your caregiving, nurturing,
responsible behaviors and spirit to the one person who can
use them the most. You will give them to the one person who
will forever cherish your gifts, which you have painfully
learned in becoming an adult daughter. You and your gifts will
create not only a person, but also a healthy sense of self
within this person. The gifts that you give will demand a
heavy price from you, for once they are given they will take
away your identity as an adult daughter. Thus, your gifts are
the ultimate that you can give. Who is the person worthy
enough to receive these gifts from you? Does anyone in the
world deserve you giving up your current identity? Only one

person is worthy of all that you can give emotionally and losing yourself in the process. She is an adult daughter herself. The person, of course, is you. Allow your adult daughter to give up herself in order to create a magnificent sense of self. The gift is from her to you—a gift of self, a gift of recovery.

You now become the creator of whom you choose to be. You now can pick up your emotional brush and paint your portrait. Your adult daughter brings all of the colors and all the paint. You bring the canvas and the idea of your image, and together you can create the healthiest self possible. You can create your life now. Do you know what you want to become? Will you pick up your brush? Will you find your self?

Getting Started

In his book *Getting Unstuck*, Sidney Simon (1988) writes about how people want to change, but can't get started. They are stuck in an emotional rut. Sometimes getting started begins when you realize that you are stuck. According to Dr. Simon, eight barriers cause people to postpone needed changes. How many of the following characteristics are holding you back?

1. **Low self-esteem**
Low self-esteem, a theme throughout this book, seems to be at the core of all the issues that we have covered. Quite simply, low self-esteem keeps us from believing that we deserve better.

2. **Not seeing alternatives**
Sometimes we do not see alternatives to our situations; other times we try many strategies to make life different,

only to find that nothing works. Eventually you might feel that you have no alternatives, or you feel a sense of learned helplessness.

3. **Not knowing what you really want**

Knowing what you want is very difficult when others have controlled you. Often adult daughters say that they don't know what to do. They are emotionally drained. However, a good starting point is becoming aware of what they *do not* want to do. Trying to figure out what you want and not knowing, especially when you are already low on energy, often adds to the sense of being stuck. The result is the "I'm so messed up I don't even know what I want to do" statement, which is also a statement of self-blame.

Knowing what you want to do is hard, but you can begin by making a list of the things that you *don't* want to do. This approach will eliminate a lot of undesirable paths for you and at least help you find a direction toward positive change. If you want to stop living the way you do now, at least you know what you don't want to do.

4. **Defending the status quo**

Do you make a lot of "but" statements? Every time you are confronted with needing to change, you agree, and then you start to say, "But . . .". These types of statements can be your reasons for not wanting to change.

5. **Fear**

You can live with many types of fear. Some fears are justified and some are mythical. Sometimes we fear finding things out about ourselves, and sometimes we fear what others might know about us. However, the fear that keeps us stuck is fear of change, like having a self-defeating behavior. You know that it is bad for you, but you keep doing it anyway. You fear what might happen if you don't engage in your usual self-defeating behavior and thus you keep repeating what you know, because the unknown scares you.

6. Lack of cooperation

Lack of cooperation occurs when you keep trying to do everything by yourself. You don't ask for help, nor do you even bother looking for it. Your isolation keeps you stuck.

7. Perfectionism

Do you believe that unless a change will be perfect and make the rest of your life perfect you don't want to make it? You hold yourself back until you believe that all the risk is gone. Usually what has gone is the opportunity to change. You can lose a lot of chances for growth and a lot of great people in your life waiting for things to be risk-free.

8. Lack of will

Surviving an alcoholic family is an emotionally exhausting experience. You just might believe that you do not have enough energy remaining to get you going. However, you don't have to do change all at once and your changes don't have to be perfect. Keep the amount of change that you advocate for yourself equal to the amount of energy that you have, and you will be more likely to start. The important thing is to start, to begin to move.

Developing Adult Resiliency Skills

Earlier in this book we talked about resiliency skills that you might have had as a child that helped you survive dysfunction and pain. Your childhood resiliency does not end when you become an adult. Resiliency is not the absence of risk or dysfunction, but rather a successful adaptation to adversity. Successfully developing resiliency depends on finding and reinforcing protective factors. When you were young, these protective factors occurred by chance. However, as an adult you can help to develop them. For example, being isolated is a risk factor, but friends and relationships in your life are protective factors. You can still use those skills from childhood, and you are now in a position to add more. If you want to become a resilient adult, you can practice developing protective factors in your life.

The following nine resiliency skills have helped other adult daughters develop protective factors in their lives and lead to recovery. Before we begin, however, consider that almost all resiliency skills are based on self-esteem. You must think enough of yourself to try new behaviors and skills. You must believe that not only can your life be different, but that it also can be better. If you do not expect much from yourself, don't expect much from others. Set your goals for yourself high— physically, emotionally and spiritually. *No one rises to low expectations!* Set the bar high and go for it!

1. **Resiliency includes knowing what you want.**

You know the kind of person you are now. If you would like to change, what would the new you look like? How would you like to feel? Would you keep some of your old emotional parts? How many new emotions would you have? Make a list of how you would like to be in your recovery. Include how you would like to live and to express your emotions, and how you can learn to receive intimacy from others. Once you have this picture, you have some idea of what recovery means for you.

2. **Resiliency includes letting go.**

You cannot hold on to the past and expect to grow in the future. You cannot keep your identity as an adult daughter as your only identity. A person in recovery is not past-oriented, but growth-oriented. As you recover you will begin to let go of pain, emotions and barriers that have held you back. Keeping these factors inside of you will usurp your energy. As you let go, you will find new energy for your recovery. What a relief and joy to let go of negative emotional baggage. The only thing that can hold you back and keep you from letting go is yourself. Recovery is yours, and you are free to let go of those things that you no longer want as part of your new self.

Letting go and resiliency go hand-in-hand; one supports the other. When you learn to let go, you are becoming resilient, and the more resilient you become the easier you will find it to let go. Additionally, letting go makes room for new feelings such as being comfortable with yourself, and others, being more accepting and loving, and having a higher self-worth and more energy.

3. **Resiliency includes balance.**

Do you remember back in chapter 9 when you identified many of your adult daughter characteristics? Recovery does not mean that you must completely change or become the exact opposite of these characteristics. Recovery means finding balance in your life. Many of the characteristics that you might consider liabilities can be changed to assets in recovery. A resilient adult daughter has balance that enables her to meet her needs, feel good about herself, care and identify with others as a healthy person, and not feel used by others. Your previous life was out of balance. Your new self is searching for balance. Your old adult daughter was willing to go to any limits to accommodate a lot of unhealthy behaviors, which kept you out of balance and a stranger to yourself. The new self knows who she is and how to maintain her balance. Don't completely throw away where you have been. Keep your strengths to keep your balance, but balance your strengths with your recovery to find yourself.

4. Resiliency includes healing.

Do not be afraid to face your pain or admit your injuries. You must heal yourself as you recover. Recovery does not include maintaining old wounds. Your healing requires you to admit injuries and perhaps forgive people who have injured you.

You need not forgive all the injuries in your life. For some victims, some events are not forgivable. However, if you choose to forgive, make your forgiving a part of your healing. Do not believe that you must forgive because someone else told you to. If you do, your forgiveness becomes codependent. Relate your forgiveness to your recovery. Ask yourself, *How will forgiving help me to heal?* When you find your answer, you will know what to do with forgiveness.

Healing and recovery both take time. Do not be too anxious. When you are injured and you return to your normal activities too soon, you risk another injury. Be patient with your recovery. The wounds are yours, and you can give them the best care possible. The healing, recovering person knows when she can move on because she is beginning to take care of herself. You cannot find recovery without going through the healing process. If you rush through it without healing through it, your old emotional wounds will call you back.

5. Resiliency includes giving.

Resiliency means that you are able to find all of the things that you have missed and then give them to yourself. Recovery is a gift of self, and many recovering people feel as if they have been emotionally reborn. They have found the gift to fully enjoy their lives. Who has your gift? You do, not on the pages of a book, but in your heart, your spirit, your emotions and your recovery.

Can you find your gift, and can you open it? Inside you are all of the things that you lost or that were taken from you when you were a little girl. Your gift is all of the things that you put in your secret emotional hiding place. Many adult daughters have been secretly carrying the gift every day, hoping each day that they could open it, only to find that one more day passed and the gift remained wrapped. Other adult daughters, like the princess in the story, have forgotten where they put their emotions and childhood spirit. Your gift has been under lock for a long time. Have you found your keys? More importantly, have you found the locks so you can let yourself out?

The keys to your recovery are inside of you. Open your locks and receive your gift. When you can give to yourself, you will find that no one can ever take the gifts away again. You will find that you will no longer hide who you are and that you will use your recovery every day. You will find that recovery is not only giving, but also the repetition of receiving. You will never grow tired of opening your gift of recovery because each day will always offer new presents. To recognize and appreciate your presents you must be recovering enough to not only know what the presents are, but also to enjoy them. When you can enjoy your gifts, you will know that you have given yourself the gift of recovery.

6. **Resiliency includes developing your sense of "self."**
How do you know not only that you are recovering, but also that you are making the transition from being only an adult daughter to developing a healthy sense of self? You will know it when you begin to believe and feel that you can be yourself without fear. You will know it when you can

celebrate yourself, when you begin to like yourself and when you can make peace with yourself. You will know that you are recovering and that you are developing a healthy sense of self when you start to do some of the following:

- You no longer feel that you must be controlling.
- You begin to have the kinds of relationships that you always wanted.
- You begin to feel more and think less about your emotions.
- You no longer fear your memories.
- You have internally made peace with people who have harmed you.
- You trust your own judgments.
- You no longer live in fear of me phobia.
- You are able to affirm your qualities.
- You no longer think of yourself only as an adult daughter.
- You are beginning to respect yourself.
- You are learning to like and love yourself.
- You can receive love and intimacy from others.
- You can say "no" to others and "yes" to yourself.
- You learn to embrace the spirit of recovery.

All of these actions and feelings are indicators of making the transition from adult daughter to becoming your own person. As you recover more, you will be closer to developing a healthy self. Recovery and developing a healthy self have one thing in common: They are both continual processes. Neither is a destination. They are both magnificent journeys. Limiting your recovery and your personal growth would be disappointing. As an adult daughter, your identity and behaviors have been restricted, but no one can restrict your growth except you.

7. **Resiliency includes learning to like yourself.**

The most devastating impact from alcoholic families is that they produce people who do not like themselves. Your greatest transition challenge will be to learn to like and love yourself. If you do not like yourself, you will find living with yourself harder than living with an alcoholic. You have proven that you can tolerate dysfunctional behavior from someone else, but you know that you will not tolerate it from yourself. When you begin to like who you are, you will open an entire emotional world that has been closed to you. Learn to like yourself. After all, you are going to spend a lot of time with the new you.

When you like yourself, you will be able to celebrate yourself as a survivor and not a victim. You will be able to enjoy humor that is not rooted in painful sarcasm. You will trust your decisions because you will like who makes them. When you like yourself, you will also respect yourself. You will improve your relationships because you will feel that you deserve the best and that you have a lot to offer. When you like yourself, you will make the transition from being a *perfect daughter* to becoming the perfect *you*, just as you are. You will realize and accept that the perfect you includes *all* of you, the positive and the negative, and that's okay. The perfect you is not codependent. The perfect you is not controlled by others. The perfect you is not afraid of herself. You are the best at being you. No more imitating someone else, and no more seeing yourself from someone else's perspective. When you like yourself, you can be yourself.

8. **Resiliency includes developing boundaries.**

Healthy boundaries are made, not born. Many adult daughters recognize their need to establish personal and professional boundaries. Many adult daughters share their fear of saying "no" to anyone. The fear of rejection keeps them from acting in their own best interests. Developing autonomy is important for adult daughters who were resilient as girls. A key to autonomy is boundaries. The resilient person no longer feels taken advantage of and does not feel used. You have a right to say "no."

Additionally, resiliency means that you know what you stand for and you feel good about your beliefs. A popular saying states that if you don't stand for something, you will fall for anything. Do you know what you stand for and what you believe? If so, you have boundaries. If not, you will need to learn more about yourself and your values.

9. **Resiliency includes learning to receive.**

Your greatest barrier to recovery and self-growth will be your inability to receive. You can try to change yourself and learn all of the processes involved, only to come face-to-face with what you have always wanted and realizing that you do not know how to accept it. Your inability to receive keeps you from becoming resilient. Break down that barrier. You cannot expect others to be able to help you if you insist on doing everything yourself. Letting others into your life and accepting their contributions takes growth. You must be able to receive what you want in order to change. If you want to feel good about yourself, you must be able to receive good feelings.

If you don't care for yourself, why not? Is something missing? Perhaps you are missing the motivation to change, not the knowledge about how to change. You must be able to receive your own motivations in order to receive from others. If you want healthy and loving relationships, are you prepared to receive love when it is offered? Can you accept a relationship with a healthy person? Joy, love, beauty, compassion and peace are gifts. Receive them. Find your keys to recovery, but more importantly, find your locks. Use your keys and open them. Throw the locks away and welcome your new life inside of you. Embrace your new life as an old friend. Welcome it home. Shout, "Let me take care of you as only I know how! Let me take care of me!" In order to grow, you will let much out, but your true growth will come from what you let in.

AFTERTHOUGHTS

What you have become is what counts.

LIZ SMITH

Experience is a good teacher, but she sends in terrific bills.

MINNA ANTRIM

*You don't get to choose how you are going to die
or when. You can only decide how you're going to live.*

JOAN BAEZ

*If you are not afraid of the voices inside you,
you will not fear the critics outside you.*

NATALIA GINZBURG

It is never too late to be what you might have been.

GEORGE ELIOT

 Postscript

We have come far on this part of our journey. I have shared it with you as far as we can go. My part of the journey is ending. Is yours beginning? I do not feel as if I have been the only writer of this book. No writing experience of mine has ever created so many emotions in me. I have been more like a painter trying to capture a picture on canvas. I hope that my vision has been clear and that I have listened well on this journey. I now pass the map on to you. You will now make your own journey. Do not forget where you have been. As painful as your road so far has been, some of the experiences will help as you travel. Learn to use the valuable ones. Some events and people may weigh you down. Let those go. You now have your choices and your map. Find your way. Find your love. Find your spirit. Find yourself.

 Appendix

The Research Behind *Perfect Daughters*

Perfect Daughters is based on two related studies of adult
daughters of alcoholic parents conducted by the author.
One study is of 125 adult daughters who offered written
responses to open-ended questions about being the daughter of an alcoholic. The topics and quotations in the book are
drawn from this "qualitative research." The other study is a
quantitative analysis of the responses to a survey, which was
self-administered to two groups of women: 624 self-identified
adult daughters of alcoholics and 585 women raised in nonalcoholic families. The statistics in the text are drawn largely
from this study.

These two complementary studies provide a comprehen-
sive description of the experiences of adult daughters of
alcoholics. The quantitative data identify the underlying
characteristics of adult daughters, and the qualitative information shows the problem areas in which these characteristics are manifested or acted out. More importantly, the
two studies offer clarification and substantiation of the

clinical observations and personal anecdotes that have, heretofore, characterized the field.

The tables in this Appendix illustrate some of the findings of the two studies and complement the text of *Perfect Daughters*. If you would like further information about the study, please contact the author at the Mid-Atlantic Addiction Training Institute, Indiana University of Pennsylvania, 1098 Oakland Avenue, Indiana, PA 15705.

Table 1. Background Differences Between ACOA Daughters and Non-ACOA Daughters

	ACOA Daughters n = 624	Non-ACOA Daughters n = 585
Background Information		
Minority	10%	10%
Married	77	74
Divorced	42	32*
Human services worker	84	89**
Drink alcohol	61	71*
Perception of Parents' Relationship*		
Poor	38%	11%
Below average	30	18
Average	20	28
Above average	11	41
Types of Abuse in Family of Origin		
Emotional abuse	80%	37%*
Child neglect	31	8*
Child physical abuse	31	9*
Child sexual abuse	19	5*
Spouse abuse	38	6*
No forms of abuse	15	58*
Emotional Satisfaction Now*		
Very low/low	20%	10%
Moderate	45	38
High/very high	34	51

*statistically significant at p ≤ .001
**statistically significant at p ≤ .05

Table 2. ACOA Daughters Compared to Non-ACOA Daughters on Dimensions and Items of the ACOA Index

	ACOA Daughters n = 624 mean (sd)	Non-ACOA Daughters n = 585 mean (sd)
Perceived Isolation	9.96 (2.40)	7.99 (2.00)
What is normal?	3.18 (.95)	2.52 (.85)
Feel different from others	3.25 (1.00)	2.73 (.87)
Difficulty with intimacy	3.53 (1.10)	2.74 (1.20)
Inconsistency	8.79 (2.40)	7.54 (1.90)
Difficulty following through	2.86 (1.10)	2.40 (.82)
Immediate gratification	3.06 (.97)	2.67 (.83)
Manage time poorly	2.87 (1.10)	2.47 (.92)
Self-Condemnation	10.72 (2.50)	8.77 (2.30)
Judge self without mercy	3.63 (1.10)	2.95 (1.00)
Difficulty having fun	3.16 (1.10)	2.44 (1.00)
Take self very seriously	3.92 (.90)	3.38 (.87)
Control Needs	6.84 (1.70)	5.54 (1.70)
Overreact to change	3.37 (.97)	2.82 (.87)
Superresponsible	3.46 (1.20)	2.72 (1.10)
Approval Needs	9.08 (2.10)	7.76 (1.80)
Seek approval and affirmation	3.51 (1.00)	3.00 (.91)
Loyal even when undeserved	3.39 (1.00)	2.98 (.98)
Lie when easy to tell the truth	2.17 (.82)	1.78 (.69)
Rigidity	8.19 (2.30)	6.75 (2.00)
Lock self into a course	2.75 (.93)	2.27 (.79)
Seek tension and crisis	2.60 (1.00)	2.09 (.87)
Avoid conflict	2.84 (1.00)	2.34 (.92)
Fear of Failure	9.58 (2.80)	7.73 (2.50)
Fear rejection and abandonment	3.03 (1.10)	2.30 (.97)
Fear criticism and judgment	3.14 (1.00)	2.64 (.94)
Fear failure	3.41 (1.10)	2.79 (1.20)
Total Score	62.13 (12.00)	52.52 (10.00)

All of the above are statistically significant at $p \leq .001$.
Scale: 5 = always, 4 = often, 3 = sometimes, 2 = seldom, 1 = never

Table 3. Problems Identified by
Adult Daughters of Alcoholics

	Percent	n = 125

Unique Problems for ACOA Daughters of Alcoholic Mothers
n = 47

Role model	45%
Relationships	36
Parenting skills	17
Identity	9
Trust	4
Other	13

Unique Problems for ACOA Daughters of Alcoholic Fathers
n = 90

Relationships	40%
Role confusion	32
Intimacy	19
Sense of self	12
Sexual abuse	7
Perfectionism	4
Other	11

Most Significant Type of Relationship Problems
n = 96

Trust	34%
Intimacy	28
Self-worth	27
Responsibility	23
Picking wrong partner	19
Other	21

Greatest Parenting Problems
n = 81

Need for control	33%
Don't know how to parent	19
Lack of consistency	16
Not able to meet child's needs	16
Other	20

Advice to Other ACOA Daughters
n = 66

Take care of yourself	30%
Get into a program	26
Use your past strengths	11
Know what you've missed	8
Associate with healthy people	6
Other	20

Note: Percentages in each category equal more than 100 because some adult daughters identified more than one problem.

 Bibliography

Ackerman, Robert J. *Abused No More: Recovery for Women from Abusive or Co-dependent Relationships*. Blue Ridge Summit, Pa.: HSI/TAB Books, Inc., 1989.

———. "Adult Daughters of Alcoholics Study." Indiana, Pa.: Indiana University of Pennsylvania, 1988.

———. *Children of Alcoholics: A Guidebook for Educators, Therapists and Parents*. Holmes Beach, Fla.: Learning Publications, 1978.

———. *Let Go and Grow: Recovery for Adult Children of Alcoholics*. Deerfield Beach, Fla.: Health Communications, Inc., 1987.

———. *Same House, Different Homes: Why Adult Children of Alcoholics Are Not All the Same*. Deerfield Beach, Fla.: Health Communications, Inc., 1987.

Ackerman, Robert J., and Edward Gondolf. "Differentiating Adult Children of Alcoholics: The Effects of Background and Treatment on ACOA Symptoms." *The International Journal of the Addictions* 26, no. 11 (1991): 1159–1172.

Ackerman, Robert J., and Susan E. Pickering. *Before It's Too Late: Helping Women in Controlling or Abusive Relationships*. Deerfield Beach, Fla.: Health Communications, Inc., 1995.

Agnew, Eleanor, and Sharon Robideaux. *My Mama's Waltz: A Book for Daughters of Alcoholic Mothers*. New York: Pocket Books, 1998.

Bass, Ellen, and Laura Davis. *The Courage to Heal*. New York: Harper and Row, 1988.

Benard, Bonnie, C. Burgoa, and K. Whealdon. *Fostering Resiliency in Kids: Protective Factors in the School*. San Francisco: Far West Laboratory, 1994.

Bepko, Claudia. *The Responsibility Trap*. New York: The Free Press, 1985.

Berkowitz, Alan, and H. Wesley Perkins. "Personality Characteristics of Children of Alcoholics." *Journal of Consulting and Clinical Psychology* 56, no. 2 (1988): 206–9.

Berman, Claire. *Adult Children of Divorce Speak Out*. New York: Simon & Schuster, 1991.

Blaker, Karen. *Born to Please*. New York: St. Martin's Press, 1988.

Braithwaite, V., and C. Devine. "Life Satisfaction and Adjustment of Children of Alcoholics: The Effects of Parental Drinking, Family Disorganization, and Survival Roles." *British Journal of Clinical Psychology* 32 (1993): 417–29.

Brenner, Avis. *Helping Children Cope with Stress*. Lanham, Md.: Lexington Books, 1984.

Butler, K. "The Anatomy of Resilience." *Family Therapy Networker* 21, no. 2 (1997): 22–31.

Cameron, Catherine. *Resolving Childhood Trauma*. Thousand Oaks, Calif.: Sage Publications, 2000.

Children of Alcoholics Foundation. *Collaboration, Coordination and Cooperation: Helping Children Affected by Parental Addiction and Family Violence*. New York: Children of Alcoholics Foundation, 1995.

Cork, Margaret R. *The Forgotten Children*. Toronto: Addiction Research Foundation, 1969.

Cowan, Connell, and Melvyn Kinder. *Smart Women, Foolish Choices*. New York: Clarkson N. Potter, Inc., 1985.

Dayton, Tian. *Trauma and Addiction*. Deerfield Beach, Fla.: Health Communications, Inc., 2000.

Earls, F., W. Reich, K. G. Jung, and C. R. Cloniger. "Psychopathology in Children of Alcoholic and Antisocial Parents." *Alcoholism: Clinical and Experimental Research* 12 (1988): 481–87.

el Guebaly, N., and D. R. Offord. "The Offspring of Alcoholics: A Critical Review." *American Journal of Psychiatry* 134, no. 4 (1997): 357–65.

Ellis, Deborah A., Robert A. Zucker, and Hiram E. Fitzgerald. "The Role of Family Influences in Development and Risk." *Alcohol Health and Research World* 21, no. 3 (1997): 218–25.

Erikson, Erik H. *Childhood and Society*. New York: W. W. Norton & Co., 1963.

Fossum, Merle. *Catching Fire*. New York: Harper and Row, 1989.

Garmezy, Norman et al., as reported by Eleanor Hoover in *Human Behavior* (April 1976).

Gondolf, Edward W., and Robert J. Ackerman. "Validity and Reliability of an Adult Children of Alcoholics Index." *The International Journal of the Addictions* 28, no. 3 (1993): 257–69.

"Having a Good Day." *USA Today*, April 13, 1989.

Hoff, Lee Ann. *People in Crisis*. 2d ed. Menlo Park, Calif.: Addison-Wesley Publishing, 1984.

Hoopes, Margaret and James Harper. *Birth Order Roles and Sibling Patterns in Individual and Family Therapy*. Rockville, Md.: Aspen Publishers Inc., 1987.

Jacobson, Sandra W. "Assessing the Impact of Maternal Drinking During and After Pregnancy." *Alcohol Health and World Research* 21, no. 3 (1997): 199–203.

Jantz, Gregory L. *Hope, Help, and Healing for Eating Disorders*. Colorado Springs, Colo.: Harold Shaw Publishers, 1995.

Johnson, J., T. Boney, and B. Brown. "Evidence of Depressive Symptoms in Children of Substance Abusers." *International Journal of the Addictions* 25, no. 4-A (1990): 465–79.

Keri Report on Confidence and the American Woman, *USA Today*, 1988.

Kumpfer, K. L. "Outcome Measures of Interventions in the Study of Children of Substance-Abusing Parents." *Pediatrics*, supplement, 103, no. 5 (1999): 1128–44.

Maine, Margo. *Father Hunger: Fathers, Daughters and Food*. Carlsbad, Calif.: Gurze Books, 1991.

Maslow, Abraham H. *Toward a Psychology of Being*. New York: John Wiley & Sons, 1968.

Morehouse, Ellen, and Tarpley Richards. "An Examination of Dysfunctional Latency Age Children of Alcoholic Parents and Problems in Intervention." *Journal of Children in Contemporary Society* 15, no. 1 (fall 1982).

Niven, R. G. "Alcohol and the Family." In *Alcoholism and Related Problems*, edited by L. J. West, 91-109. Englewood Cliffs, N.J.: Prentice-Hall, 1984.

Norwood, Robin. *Women Who Love Too Much*. Los Angeles: Jeremy P. Tarcher, Inc., 1985.

Obuchowska, I. "Emotional Contact with the Mother as a Social Compensatory Factor in Children of Alcoholics." *International Mental Health Research Newsletter* 16, no. 4 (1974): 2:4.

Perrin, Thomas W. "I Am an Adult Child of an Alcoholic." Thomas W. Perrin, 1984.

Reid, J., P. Macchetto, and S. Foster. "No Safe Haven: Children of Substance Abusing Parents." Center on Addiction and Substance Abuse at Columbia University, 1999.

Rivinus, T. M., D. Levoy, M. Matzko, and R. Seifer. "Hospitalized Children of Substance Abusing Parents and Sexually Abused Children: A Comparison." *Journal of the American Academy of Child and Adolescent Psychiatry* 31, no. 6 (1992): 1019–1923.

Robinson, Bryan E., and J. Lyn Rhoden. *Working with Children of Alcoholics.* 2d ed. Thousand Oaks, Calif.: Sage, 1998.

Sanford, Linda Tschirhart. *Women and Self-Esteem.* Lecture presented at Indiana University of Pennsylvania, Indiana, Pa., April 1988.

Sanford, Linda Tschirhart, and Mary Ellen Donovan. *Women & Self-Esteem.* New York: Anchor Press/Doubleday, 1985.

Seilhamer, R., T. Jacob, and N. Dunn. "The Impact of Alcohol Consumption on Parent-Child Relationships in Families of Alcoholics." *Journal of Studies on Alcohol* 54, no. 2 (1993): 189–98.

Seixas, Judy, and Geraldine Youcha. *Children of Alcoholism.* New York: Crown Publishing, 1985.

Sheehy, Gail. *Passages: Predictable Crises of Adult Life.* New York: E. P. Dutton, 1978.

Sher, K. J. *Children of Alcoholics: A Critical Appraisal of Theory and Research.* Chicago: University of Chicago Press, 1991.

———. "Psychological Characteristics of Children of Alcoholics." *Alcohol Health and Research World* 21, no. 3 (1997): 247–53.

Simon, Sidney B. *Getting Unstuck.* New York: Warner Brothers, 1988.

Subby, Robert. *Lost in the Shuffle.* Deerfield Beach, Fla.: Health Communications, Inc., 1987.

Tower, Cynthia Crosson. *Understanding Child Abuse and Neglect.* 3d ed. Boston: Allyn and Bacon, 1996.

Volchok, Susan. "Childhood Labels." *Glamour,* July 1985.

Wallerstein, J. S. "Children of Divorce: Stress and Developmental Tasks." In N. Garmezy and M. Rutter (eds.), *Stress, Coping and Development in Children* (pp. 265–302). New York: McGraw-Hill, 1983.

Werner, E. E. "Resilient Offspring of Alcoholics: A Longitudinal Study from Birth to Age 18." *Journal of Studies on Alcohol* 47, no. 1 (1986): 34–40.

Werner, E. E., and J. L. Johnson. "The Role of Caring Adults in the Lives of Children of Alcoholics." *Children of Alcoholics: Selected Readings* 2 (2000).

Williams, Carol N. "Differences in Child Care Practices Among Families with Alcoholic Fathers, Alcoholic Mothers, and Two Alcoholic Parents." Abstract in *Dissertation Abstracts International* 44 (1983): 299–A.

Wilsnack, R. W., S. C. Wilsnack, and A. D. Klassen. "Women's Drinking and Drinking Problems: Patterns from a 1981 National Survey." Paper presented at the Annual Meeting of the Society for the Study of Social Problems, San Francisco, September 1982.

Windle, Michael. "Concepts and Issues in COA Research." *Alcohol and Health Research World* 21, no. 3 (1997): 185–91.

Woititz, Janet G. *Adult Children of Alcoholics*. Deerfield Beach, Fla.: Health Communications, Inc., 1983.

Wolin, S. and S. Wolin. *The Resilient Self: How Survivors of Troubled Families Rise Above Adversity*. New York: Random House, 1993.

Zelditch, Morris. "Role Differentiation in the Nuclear Family: A Comparative Study." In *Family, Socialization and Interaction Process*, edited by Talcott Parsons and R. Bales. 307–51. Glencoe, Ill.: Free Press, 1955.

 Index

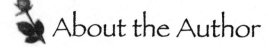 About the Author

Robert J. Ackerman, Ph.D., is professor of sociology at Indiana University of Pennsylvania and director of the Mid-Atlantic Addiction Training Institute. He is a cofounder of the National Association for Children of Alcoholics. He is the author of twelve books and has received numerous awards. His work has been featured extensively in the media including *CNN Headline News, Today, Oprah, Newsweek* and *The New York Times.* He and his wife Kimberly have three children and live in Indiana, Pennsylvania.

NOTES